The Uncorrupted Life
of An Old Bladed Putter

A collection of golfing fables

By

JAMES ELLIS-CAIRD

ILLUSTRATED BY JAMIE BUCKRIDGE

THE CHOIR PRESS

First published in the United Kingdom in 2022 by
The Choir Press

Paperback: ISBN 978-1-78963-322-1
Hardback: ISBN 978-1-78963-323-8

Dedication

To my Dad, A truly wonderful man with a truly
dreadful short game

*Golf can best be defined as an endless series of tragedies
obscured by the occasional miracle.'*

Anonymous

*'A centipede was happy quite, until a toad in fun
Said pray, which leg comes after which?
That raised his doubts to such a pitch
He fell distracted into a ditch
Not knowing how to run.'*

Katherine Craster, Pinafore Poems, 1871

Contents

Acknowledgments

Thankyou to my wonderful wife Helen. The edits may have been brutal and the feedback harsh, but you were the one who focused me, inspired me and turned my ramblings into a collection of golfing fables of which I am immensely proud.

Thankyou to Jamie, you've captured the essence of my words in your beautiful pictures and it's been lovely to work with an old friend.

And finally, I want to thank my Mum for being a constant, warm, supportive and loving presence in my life.

Preface

When you really think about it, it sounds pretty silly ... to have had a love affair my entire life with a game which at base, is about smacking a small white ball around a field with the object of getting it into little round holes. It's hardly profound, barely sensible, maybe it is after all the 'ruination of a good walk' as Mark Twain once complained. So how can I possibly justify the countless hours I've spent practicing, or the weeks and months I've spent hoofing my little bag full of clanky clubs around miles of the British countryside? Or indeed the career I've forged helping others to do the same?

I don't know, maybe I can't on any objective measure. But somehow, it doesn't feel like wasted time, or a wasted journey ... As I look back over a lifetime of golf, a myriad of memories rise before me ... The time my friend caddied for me in the open qualifier, and the weather was so bad we could hardly stand ... we carded an eleven on the second, our umbrella broke on the third, our shoes squelched by the forth, but we battled on laughing and crying only missing the cut by two shots. Or the time I was playing on my own one summer's evening and came face to face with a great deer, stock still, staring, both shocked by the aliveness of the other for one brief but eternal second, before with a bound he was gone into the woods. Or the elicit kiss I shared with my girlfriend in the dunes of a famous links course, before emerging to resume our round under the disapproving eyes of a ladies' four-ball. The rare holes in ones, the millions of practiced putts, the clubs I've broken, the all-too-common mis-hits and misses ... They're all wonderful to me, knitting together to create a fabric of memories, learnings and experiences that represent not just a game of golf, but my life.

In my teens golf lifted me out of adolescent angst and gave me focus, in my twenties it gave me aspiration and purpose, in my thirties it gave me a passion for teaching, and now, more than at any point in my life, it gives me joy. I can't really explain it, I guess anything you do with care and attention over and over again can become joyful, elevating it beyond a collection of motions to a kind of 'practice'. The sound of the club whipping through the air, the particular note the ball makes when it's hit soundly and the rip of the wind as it courses through the air, these things give me great pleasure ... far more than where the ball lands or what my final score might be. There's a beauty in the doing of golf – in the pinpoint focus and concentration as I conjure up a match-winning shot from an impossible lie, or figure out how to get my ball onto the green from deep in the trees. I'm nowhere else but right there, just me and the ball and the course. My life could be falling apart, and at times it has, but the course has always been there, to distract, to soothe and also to find that clarity and stillness of complete focus that takes you beyond yourself and gives a break from the mundanities and struggles of the everyday.

Golf has also brought me up, taught me a thing or two about how to be an adult ... hitting my ball into the bunker after the eighth time of trying, duffing another tee shot along the ground, holding my nerve in a tight match – I've learnt about patience, about perseverance, about bad luck and good and how my mood can create both, about letting things go and moving on. Golf can highlight the worst of us, but with practice, I think it's also brought out the best in me, not just on the golf course, but off – when my son wants to play the same dinosaur battle game for the hundredth time, when my wife critiques my lovingly prepared and presented roast dinner, when we moved house, struggled to have a baby, when my father died. It's golf I've drawn on to find my strengths and to renew them.

So yes, golf maybe is a good walk ruined for some, but for me, it's been a good life lived.

In this little book I hope that I can convey something of what golf means to me, of what I've learnt, and what I've unlearnt. I want to share the stories of the amazing clients that I've had the pleasure to work with for over twenty years, as well as some of my own.

And in so doing, I want to loosen the game of golf from the shackles of expectation, which drill us to manufacture a 'perfect' swing, count each shot and follow every rule. That's not all that golf is about – it never was and it never should be – it's about spending time with a friend you don't get to see very often, smelling fresh cut grass on a dewy morning, bracing yourself against a west wind, feeling your head lift and your shoulders unclench as you walk down the first and the small triumph of a ball eventually finding a hole.

Whether you've never even considered the stuffy old sport, are just taking it up, are a seasoned pro or are about to give up the bloody game, I hope the collection of fables in this book will touch you in some way, and maybe allow you to see the game anew.

CHAPTER ONE

The Classic, the Gentle and the Wild

A tribute to the golf course

I head out to my local club early in the evening, the sun's rays have begun to recede, and the course is relaxing and softening. Rabbits and birds are once again colonising the fairways as the golfing traffic recedes to a trickle. I shoulder my small bag and set off down the first, hearing the soft jangling of my clubs intermingled with the birds, a dog and a distant airplane far above, scudding through the haze of approaching dusk. I'm struck by the soft beauty of the place, the mingling of a multitude of greens and yellows, water and hill contrasting starkly with the scarlet red of the flag flapping idly

1

in the distance. My heart lifts to be outside, to be part of nature, to breathe fresh air. I can feel my shoulders loosening, my lungs expanding and my stride lengthening as the cares of the day melt into the soft grass of the fairway.

I can't think of another sport where a good place to start one's story would be talking about the surface on which it is played. It's difficult to wax lyrical about the beauty of the concrete baseball court, the majesty of the swimming pool ... some have tried tapping into the 'hallowed ground' of the football pitch, but what have you really got to work with here? A rectangle of flat grass, fringed by stands? Come on! But the golf course ... that is an entirely different proposition. Golf courses long ago transcended their status as a 'surface' and are today as much a part of the fabric of our landscape as the patchwork of fields, woods, streams, hills and lakes that characterise the British countryside.

At best, they are in and of themselves a thing of beauty, a way of conserving and protecting the countryside, providing sanctuary for animal and plant life, and a resource for the community. They can provide us with a kind of passport to nature giving us permission to walk, to breathe and to decompress in a way that many people wouldn't take up without the allure of hitting a little white ball. They have the ability to take my breath away with their raw beauty, to soothe me with their undulating fairways, and inspire with their swooping vistas.

So, remember next time you're on the course to look up from you're score card, to shift your focus from playing to being, and take a look around you.

From the manicured perfection of Augusta to the raw, wild beauty of Royal North Devon, no two golf courses are the same. In fact, they are as different and unique as we are, with their own personalities, eccentricities and challenges – some demanding precision, others power, others an elemental battle, and I think they all have something to offer. If I go too long playing crisp, smart country club courses then I crave something rawer – a links course that will buffet me out of myself and cast me away, but then I find myself comforted to return to something more relaxing like a little woodland course, with a friendly club house to welcome me at the end. I think it's a question of balance, each kind of course has it merits, suiting a particular mood, stage of life or goal. But the richness of the game comes from its diversity. The thing is, if you haven't experienced something, you don't necessarily know what you're missing ...

Take Mike for example. As a fund manager at a big international bank he played all his golf on corporate days at some of the most prestigious courses in the world. In the four years I'd known him, the lucky man had played Pebble Beach, Spyglass Hill, Wentworth, Woburn and Stoke Park to name just a few.

Mike was a self-proclaimed 'summer golfer' who wouldn't touch his clubs during the winter months. For the past few years the routine would be the same: mid-march, he'd come into the warm and cosy comforts of *Urban Golf* and take six lessons with me – what he called his 'thawing-out' process before the corporate golf season began.

Last March though, Mike seemed a little apprehensive. He told me that his wife had booked a special golfing trip to Scotland for his fiftieth birthday, but that he was playing what in his words were *some obscure forsaken* courses rather than the classic St Andrews and Loch Lomonds' that he'd expected. *Some place called Macrahants or something*? He was only referring to Machrihanish, one of the most beautiful courses in the world. I talked effusively about the wonders of this hidden gem, but Mike was unconvinced. *Never heard of it*, he complained. I told him to at least keep an open mind, and saw him off, smiling to myself … I was convinced that this holiday would give him a whole new experience of what it means to play golf.

Up until this point, all Mike had known of golf was the immaculate perfection of the corporate golf world, playing golf as part of business four balls, on courses with a succession of other business four balls, being sent out every eight minutes with military precision. For Mike, golf was pressurised: keep up with the group in front, walk fast, play straight and make good small talk on the way round. It's not that Mike didn't enjoy this way of playing – he did, very much – but it wasn't exactly 'fun'. This kind of golf doesn't allow the chance to experiment, learn, take a few 'celebrity drops', look at the beauty around you or reminisce with a close friend. I don't know if you've seen the photos of a long line of mountaineers queuing to reach the summit of Everest? But I think playing these famous courses has a parallel. Yes, you're out playing/climbing the best/ tallest in the world, but the magic is dimmed when that becomes an overcrowded, pressurised experience, to be conquered or ticked off rather than experienced and relished. Particularly when there are so many other wonderful mountains out there.

A couple of days after Mike and his wife departed to Scotland, I received a text that I'll never forget. It was a picture of the normally refined and tidy Mike, his arms held aloft, rain plastering his sports jacket, his hair standing straight up in the wind and a wild smile on his face. Behind him was the raw beauty of Machrihanish, not a soul in sight, just the first tee, the beach and the fairway. Three words accompanied it … *This is golf!* From that holiday on, Mike has played all sorts of golf courses … he's even played in the winter.

I love all sorts of golf courses: wild, refined, gentle – and choosing a favourite would be impossible. So, I haven't. Indulge me if you will, because I've chosen three instead. They're not necessarily the best courses in the UK by any objective standard, although I do think they are all objectively wonderful, but what makes them my favourites is something beyond the physical courses … it's the special moments that I've had playing these courses that I'll never forget. So drum roll please … here they are.

Disclaimer: I want to apologise to all the courses I haven't had the chance to mention. You're all brilliant in your own ways!

Wild simplicity

I've always loved the simple things in life – a bbq on the beach, a thermos of tea with egg sandwiches, swimming in the sea – and so the holiday that my wife and I took to Muasdale, Kintyre on the western peninsula of Scotland was pretty much perfect. We stayed in a little caravan opposite a beautiful, rugged beach with the plan to do a bit of surfing and play a few rounds of golf, including the extraordinary Machrihanish golf club.

On the second to last day of our trip, the day dawned

warm and dry. I love the emptiness of that first light of the day, so got up early and sat on the steps of our caravan with a cup of tea looking out at the sea. There, right in our little bay, I spotted two seals playing between the rocks. It thrilled me and gave me a craving to be in the water, so I insisted we start the day with a surf at Westport beach, a stunning, wide bay where the waves roll smoothly in to crash on the shoreline. Now I'm rather pushing the meaning of 'surf' here. 'Being thrown around like washing in a machine' would be a more accurate description. But it was worth it for those rare few seconds when we did catch a wave and stayed on the board long enough to feel the effortless energy of the wave whisking us towards the beach. My wife beat her all-time record of nine seconds on the board that morning. She jumped off cheering and whooping before we wrapped up in towels and drank hot tea in the dunes.

We hadn't got any fixed plans of where to play golf that afternoon, so we pulled a map and studied the peninsula ... noticing a golf-course-shaped patch on the very tip jutting out towards Arran, marked *Carradale Golf Club*. After hot showers and more tea, we slung our clubs in the back of the car and headed out on a beautiful road trip, cutting round the craggy coast, the sun bouncing off the white waves as they hit the water soaked black rocks.

After an hour of the twisting, turning road, passing only occasional clusters of houses, their backs arched against the bracing wind, we arrived at the deserted Carradale Golf Club. We changed our shoes in the carpark without fear of a headmaster-type figure telling us off, left a tenner in the honesty box, and headed out.

Carradale Golf Club is a nine-hole course, founded in 1906 and positioned on the east coast of the Kintyre peninsula. Seven of the nine wonderful holes are less than 300 yards in length – a far cry from the modern-day brutes of 480-yard-plus par-fours. But don't be fooled, this course is no cinch. If you think you can blast your driver at every hole, then you had better be straight, lucky or take a few celebrity drops, because this natural heath and moorland course is flooded with outcrops of rock and heather ready to offer even a really good drive a wild and unforgiving bounce.

We started confidently up the hill of the modest par-three, and as we reached the higher ground of the first green, the wonder of the place really hit us. With the fresh scent of the sea in the air, and the seagulls crying hauntingly, the views out across the sea towards the Isle of Arron were to die for.

It's moments like these when the landscape can just elevate and inspire your game, and even though the course guide wouldn't have suggested a driver as the club of choice on the second tee, we couldn't help ourselves. Maybe it was the beauty of the hole that helped calm and clear our minds, I don't know, but we both hit lovely long drives that somehow managed to miss the awaiting scrub of purple and blue heather tantalisingly calling to our balls.

I tend to walk slower after a good tee shot, I guess it's because I'm not in any hurry to fix a problem and like to savour the feeling. But on this occasion, it wasn't just the lovely shots we'd hit, it was the view, the sun and wind on our faces, the quiet that we wanted to last forever. I stood on the sparse wild green, soaking up the moment, allowing my mind to drift over the beauty all around me. I may not have matched my wife's birdie, but no matter, this was a hole I wouldn't forget.

We reached the sixth, the signature 'pudding bowl', so named because of its steeply angled sides. I wandered along the narrow heather-lined path to the back tees, teetering right on the top edge of the cliff, with nothing between me and the Atlantic. I called my wife to join me and we stood still, silent, transfixed by the miles and miles of green grey sea undulating far below us, framed on every side by the tall, craggy cliffs of Carradale. A tiny bay glinting with white sand and shells nestled to our right, ringed by the gentle puff of smoke from the house overlooking it. The evening sun shone softly, lending a pinkish warmth to the roughhewn country and a haze to the sea. We sat down on the coarse grass, not ready to tear our eyes away. I got out the thermos, refilled this time with a wee dram and we sat happily, the strong liquor warming our insides as we watched the sun slip towards the horizon. A truly magical course, a truly magical day.

Walking in the footsteps of golfing greats

I spent a happy five years at Hazlemere Golf Club completing my PGA training. The head pro was very relaxed and gave us assistants a good deal of freedom – only some of which we misspent. I had a flexible working week, choosing my own hours and lording it in my vast amounts of free time practicing and playing golf. One of the best things for me about training at Hazlemere was how friendly it was. Even now, when I go back to visit for a few holes on a Sunday evening, there will undoubtably be smiling faces from the past seated round the bar after their game. I love that feeling of warmth and familiarity – it makes you feel places like *Cheers* really do exist.

One member in particular took me under his wing and looked after me, and over the years became a good friend. John was twenty-five years my senior and someone I looked up to and admired. He was a generous man, and lived life to the full, both on and off the course. He loved his golf and the relaxed and sociable atmosphere at Hazlemere, and was also a member of the prestigious Wentworth golf club in Surrey, where he played less often, saving his rounds for special occasions.

As a young aspiring professional, Wentworth represented to me the pinnacle of golfing excellence, the crème de la crème, the golfing elite, and I knew each vista and curve of that course in detail, having watched tournaments on TV and visited to see the pros in person. And so, you can imagine how incredibly excited I was when John invited me and two friends to play the west course. Not only that, we were to play one day after the end of the BMW PGA championship, hosted that year at Wentworth. We were literally going to be treading in the footsteps of my golfing heroes.

It was John's fiftieth birthday, so to add to the occasion, he had arranged for us to be driven there by his chauffeur and have dinner in the club house after. I was barely twenty-five and quite sheltered, so this extravagance seemed outrageously glamorous to me, and I loved every moment. We arrived early for a champagne breakfast, then headed down a wide corridor lined with mahogany wood and adorned with the clubs of past winners to the locker rooms. And what a locker room it was. No smell of old socks and mud here – only polished leather and wealth. I distinctly remember wishing that I'd asked my mother to iron my trousers as I sheepishly tried to make myself look presentable in one of the long bedevilled mirrors. After a nervy practice, we headed to the first tee. And there it was, Wentworth, stretching out before us in all its manicured beauty. It looked larger than life – set on a huge estate fringed by vast mansions, the fairways looked extravagantly wide and long, the tee boxes huge and intimidating, the bunkers enormous and perfectly raked. I was truly awe struck by its benevolent magnificence, which may go some way to explain why only one of us hit the fairway that morning and it wasn't me – but at least I didn't top 50 yards like my friend.

As we strode up the middle of the first fairway, I had a strange sense of deja vu, in some ways I knew this course so well, but to play it was brand new. I guess this must be what it's like meeting a big celebrity, a strange mix of familiarity and novelty. I imagined the crowds that only yesterday had lined the beautiful striped fairways to witness the battle between the best players in the world, sharing for a brief moment these golfers' joy, exhilaration and crushing defeat as they progressed around this classic course. I could almost hear the roars still echoing as crucial putts were holed, fairways found and bunkers vanquished.

As we reached the first green, it struck me that I had never putted on greens that were so smooth, short and fast. I'd played courses with good greens, but these had been prepared to accommodate the tournament and were at a different level … I could understand why commentators talk of *putting on glass* as I duly sent my first putt a good 10 feet past. After a couple of holes and a few awkward putting strokes I began to be able to better read the greens and found it easier than putting on the slower greens I was used to – I'm clearly suited to fine things.

My shot of the day was a four-iron up the hill to the par-three fourteenth, which finished two or three inches from the hole. There weren't the thousands there to see and applaud it, but I did get a 'golfers clap' from a local dog walker as we approached the green.

Waiting to tee off on the fifteenth, I was pulled back to the memory of standing at this exact hole the previous year, on tiptoe, waiting to get my first glimpse of Tiger playing in person. I'd arrived early to get a good spot, and along with fifty or so others stood waiting, the anticipation growing as we heard the distant applause grow closer, and felt the energy as Tiger and the huge crowd following him submerged the fifteenth tee box. I watched him intently as he smiled and tipped his cap to acknowledge us, before he focused on the fairway with an intensity that crackled. As he elegantly took his golfing position, the world fell deadly still. No one moved, no one spoke, even the birds seemed to respect this short moment and fell silent. A second later Tiger's club rose upwards and then a whip crack as his swing tore through the small white ball. I didn't watch its flight, the roars and applause of the crowd said enough – my eyes were still on Woods as he effortlessly turned into his signature finish position.

Finding myself back in the present, I stepped up to play my own shot, bringing all that I had learnt from Tiger to my game, and played my best drive of the day. I even acknowledged the roars of the imaginary crowds with Tiger's customary nod of the head and tight smile as I followed my friends up the fairway. I hope nobody noticed.

We decided to take the pressure off ourselves to keep

score, instead playing a friendlier four-ball match. It was fun but still competitive, John's experience winning out on the par-five seventeenth. This is Wentworth's signature hole. A long sweeping dogleg that goes down, around, up and eventually back down towards the green. It's a beautiful tree-lined, demanding hole, requiring three of your best shots to get to the green.

As we putted out on the eighteenth, the grand-stands still up around us, I couldn't help pausing to take it all in. I felt so incredibly lucky and grateful to get a chance to play here ... I think it's a wonderful thing about golf that the vast majority of the top courses are accessible to the public. Imagine the equivalent in other sports and getting to play at Old Trafford, Wimbledon or Lords, it would be unheard of apart from for a privileged few. So, as I picked up my ball, shook hands with my friends and thanked John for the opportunity, I remember feeling just a deep and uncomplicated sense of satisfaction and happiness. Even at this early stage in my career, I was clear that I hadn't the competitive instinct to play at an elite level, but if a career in golf opened up the possibility to be in amongst it, to be part of something this wonderful, I knew it was the job for me.

A round with my dad

Perhaps not as extreme as the links courses or as refined as the prestigious courses, the gentler parkland courses that lie up and down the country can be just as wonderful in their own ways. Living in Buckinghamshire I am spoilt for choice, but one of my favourites has got to be Harewood Downs, where I was a member for a few years before turning pro-fessional. It's a warm, friendly club, which accommo-dated us younger golfers with pleasure rather than tolerating us as some of the bigger clubs tend to do. The seventeenth is where I got my first hole in one – I hit a 110-yard pitching wedge up to the pretty green which to my delight pitched a few feet past the flag before spinning back into the hole. It's also where I won the club championship, accompanied by my best friend as caddy – he'd had rather a rough night before the tournament, and was feeling a bit worse for wear and made some pretty rash calls, *Don't lay up, mate, go straight over the trees, forget the lie, just mash it on the green.* The result was I played a far more bombastic round than I'd ever had the confidence to do before, and it worked and we won, evidence of the true worth of a caddy, however inebriated.

But although Harewood is one of my favourites, the course I hold closest to my heart is the relaxed, gentle and beautiful Ley Hill Golf Club. Officially formed back in 1919 it had no pro shop, no pro, no practice range when I joined, and to this day, being set on common land means that it's completely open to the public. So, on a Sunday afternoon you often share the second fairway with children playing football, the odd cricket ball hit for six from the quintessentially English cricket pitch over the road and have the support of punters from the local pub sitting around the tee. It's not 'perfect' in the technical sense of the word ... the greens are cut with a hand mower and can have a bit of bobble, and the fairways are not as tightly maintained as the 'posher' courses, but honestly that's not what matters. Ley Hill is a beautiful, natural set of nine holes that tightly twist and turn up and down through an old wood, and are truly a part of the local community. And don't let my description lure you into a false sense that this makes Ley Hill an easy option ... I've certainly spent more time in the trees than on the fairway – it's a course that can improve your game as a pro as well as being a perfect place to learn if you're a beginner, it's truly for everyone. And for me, it's a very special place ... there are as many of my lost balls in the undergrowth as there are memories, and the round I had there with my dad is one that I cherish the most.

My dad was a very hard-working family man, and devoted himself to providing for my mum, me and my sisters. In fact, he never really stopped working, and after retiring from business he set up as a 'handyman' and loved driving round in his small white van to build cupboards, decorate, garden and have a tea, biscuit and chat with his devoted customers. And in his spare time, us children kept him busy painting, decorating and maintaining all of our homes, as well of course with a growing brood of grandchildren and later great grandchildren.

So, it's perhaps not surprising that my dad didn't have much time for hobbies earlier in his life, but he did take up golf in his sixties, and it became a real passion for him. I gave him a few lessons at my club and off he went, firstly playing at the local public courses before joining Hazlemere Golf Club, which was closer to home.

He wasn't interested in club politics or entering into the club competitions. He was far happier playing either on his own or with his friend Cedric. He avoided the crowds and would zip round the course proudly in just under three hours, have a coffee and then head home to cook supper for my mum. He was wonderfully enthusiastic about the game and I would often get a call from him to clarify a particular ruling that had come up in his game or to give me a detailed run down of his latest score card. He never really practiced and had a wonderfully unique swing and a chipping style that gave me the shivers, but it didn't matter to him. His goal was never to improve or perfect his swing, but to enjoy it, and if there was any improvement it would be done through playing the game in the way he wanted.

Like most regular golfers though, every now and then his swing would stop 'working' and the whole thing would feel more awkward, more effortful and less powerful, leaving him stumped as to what had happened. In the case of my dad, like so many regular non-internet 'tip searching' golfers, it would be something simple, and usually ten minutes in the garden with me would have the problem diagnosed and remedied. A habit for my dad was to creep further and further away from the ball and allow his ball position to move too far forward in his stance. It would happen in such small increments over a period of rounds that it would be difficult for him to notice, and his swing would still be able to accommodate. After a while though, there would come a tipping point when his swing couldn't adapt any further and the whole thing would collapse. I very much enjoyed helping him out at these times ... getting far too much credit for being a life saver by just realigning him back into his normal stance. His swing would improve and after one or two rounds his game would be back.

My dad was ever so proud of me for being a professional, and although I'd feign embarrassment when he talked about me, it was actually very important to me knowing I'd made him proud. But regardless of how proud he was, he never really seemed to want to play golf with me. I'm not really sure why, perhaps he was embarrassed by his game or didn't think I wanted to play with him? I hope not. Whatever the reason, we eventually managed to arrange our first game and decided to play at Ley Hill. Funny thing was it didn't seem to be my dad who felt most of the pressure that day, but me. I think I was trying too hard to impress or live up to his expectations. I hit right into the trees on the first, out of bounds left at the second, a dreadful shot at the third that somehow found the green, and again found the trees on the right at the fourth. It wasn't my best start … but as we went round, the course practically to ourselves, so quiet and peaceful, it seemed to offer us the opportunity to be a bit different together. We began to talk and then to chat in a way we hadn't done before, and the more we relaxed the better we played, enjoying our own and each other's games. As we putted out on the last green the course was a little busier, a few people grabbing the chance after work to enjoy a few holes in the late summer evening. We shook hands and sat outside for a drink and just kept talking. I don't remember exactly what we talked about, it probably wasn't particularly profound, but I'll always remember it as the day I became a friend as well as a son to my dad.

Time is a precious commodity and golf on a gentle course like Ley Hill can somehow slow things down, giving space and time to think, to breathe, to talk. Use it how you wish … it might be to find yourself, to find your game or perhaps, like me that day, to find your dad.

Our last game together was at Stoke Park golf club in 2013 for his seventieth birthday – I miss him every day.

CHAPTER TWO

The Joys of Imperfection

Learning to play 'good enough' golf

In the 1950s a British psychoanalyst called Donald Winnicott introduced the idea of a 'good enough mother'. He understood the incredible pressure placed on parents, even in those days, to be 'perfect', to never make mistakes, to do it all. Winnicott recognised that in fact all children really need are parents that love them and do their best.

Now more than ever, we need the concept of 'good enough', not just in our parenting, but in our wider lives. It seems that we aspire to superhuman levels of perfection in all that we do. And golf is no exception. The single most important thing I've learnt about the game is that you really only need to be 'good enough' to play well and enjoy yourself. Those occasional perfect shots are a joy and bonus, but they're not what get us round the course. It's the shots that weren't quite what we wanted, but still take us closer to the hole, the shots from the rough that put us back on the fairway, the putts that guarantee we get it in next time – these are the bread and butter of golf, the real heroes of the game.

A few years ago now I had the pleasure to teach a highly successful businesswoman, Lin, who was new to the game, but determined to 'conquer' golf in the same way that she had triumphed in the business world. I admired her passion and commitment, and loved hearing her stories of international business trips, meetings at the highest level and determination to break through the glass ceiling she saw imposed on many of her female colleagues. That said, the golf was not going particularly well.

In our first few lessons at *Urban Golf* we worked on swinging the club naturally and fluidly, to begin to get a sense of the feeling of the motion. It was all going very well, until we introduced the ball. As I'd expect, her first shots were pretty haphazard, but she quickly improved, and more shots were heading down the fairway. I was more than satisfied with her progress. In fact, it was clear she had potential to be a nice golfer. But unfortunately, that wasn't how Lin saw it. Her mis-hits were met with angry frustration and her 50-yard drives with derision. Even our time spent practicing putting was fraught with her chastisement of herself when her ball failed to find the hole. It seemed to me that she was incredibly hard on herself, particularly given her short time learning the game. She told me that she had always been a sporty person and could normally pick up technique quickly, and was incredibly frustrated that she wasn't mastering the game. Although I admired her enthusiasm, it was clear to me that her high expectations were impacting her ability to learn and certainly to enjoy the game.

I explained to her that it was absolutely impossible in a game like golf to get it right 100% of the time, and added, with some trepidation, that it was important for all golfers to be at peace with imperfection. Now imperfection is something a lot of my clients find difficult to sit with. We expect perfection from ourselves in so many ways, from our appearance, to our grades in school, to our job performance, that it is perhaps second nature for my clients to bring this expectation with them to the game of golf. And unfortunately, in my experience, this is often reinforced by the style of perfectionistic and technique-driven teaching. But perfection really isn't the key to golf.

My reasoning here, I explained to Lin, is that we are not machines; no human can reproduce the same movement every time, and in a game like golf, which is both non-reactive and incredibly variable, playing 'perfectly' is a fantasy. You only need to watch a giant of the game like Tiger Woods to see how few shots in even a superb round turn out exactly how he'd hoped.

Instead, I continued, I like to think about the game as something that is alive. At this point I could tell that she was starting to think I was a little mad. But there was a good reason for thinking about it in this way. Living things don't reproduce the same behaviour again and again. They adapt, they evolve, they take into account their contexts. And this is a great thing, no machine could hook a golf ball up and out of the deep rough, or from behind a tree. Aspiring for inflexible perfection deadens the game in the same way as making a butterfly flap its wings uniformly with each motion.

But that's not all. An engineered perfect game deadens our ability to respond to our environment, and it also takes away the uniquely human quality of emotion. Golf is played with the mind as well as the body: it's the mind that means even the world's best golfers can miss a 4ft putt under extreme pressure, but also how tournaments are miraculously won from seven shots down. If we are too focused on getting it right all the time, we risk lobotomising this natural resource which allows us to take risks, improvise, as well as our ability to play creatively, to play resourcefully and most importantly to play with joy.

So, I went on, if we learn with expectations of reaching perfection, we are putting our time and energy into a mirage. At best, we will end up with a fragile and brittle game that is likely to 'break down' under the pressure of a real golf course, and at worst the frustration and broken expectations of this elusive goal are likely to drive us away from the game.

And so, even if it were possible for someone to perfectly manufacture and secure a 'picture-perfect' game, whilst maintaining their sanity at the end of the process, I honestly don't believe it would ever fully capture all that is necessary to play and enjoy the game. As Voltaire once said, 'Don't let the perfect be the enemy of the good.'

With my rant about perfection now over, Lin and I resolved to start again, with new expectations to guide us. We agreed to focus again on how each shot 'felt' rather than on where it landed, to think of a non-perfect shot as setting a challenge from which she could learn and grow her game, and lastly to focus on celebrating the wonderful moments, even if these were more luck than judgement. Over the next six lessons, I helped Lin to stay focused on what she could control, not what she couldn't control, to find joy in the good moments, to hold hope in the bad moments. With time and patience, her game became more consistent, more reliable, and by our sixth lesson she was ready for the golf course. Her game wasn't perfect by any means, but it was good enough.

When we said goodbye at the end of our time together, Lin recalled to me my so-called 'rant' and remembered what a relief it was to her to be able to let go of the perfectionism that was demanded of her in so many areas of her life. Instead, she said that golf for her was fun! I couldn't have hoped for a more ringing endorsement than that.

CHAPTER THREE

The Day I Holed Three Bunker Shots

Learning through playing

Just the other day, I met up with a friend of mine in a lovely little brassiere in Soho. Probably twenty years my senior and someone who has spent most of his life living and working in London, I always look forward to our meetings and his many tales of life, the universe, books and film. He's also a keen golfer and student of the game for the past thirty years. And so, at some point in our conversation, we normally get to talk about our shared love of the game.

On this particular afternoon, the topic of golf was at the top of the agenda as he just couldn't wait to tell me about one of his golfing buddies who after thirty years of playing golf, happened to show a video of his swing to his wife. Her cool response was to say, *Now there's me thinking you were out playing golf all these years.*

Watching the video, I can assure you this man's swing was not pretty! It was quick, whippy and had little in common with the textbook professional swing. And so, if I were his wife, I'd also have questioned his true whereabouts over the past thirty years on those Wednesday and Friday afternoons.

Joking aside though, I'm actually as much of a fan of the more eccentric looking golf swing as the elegant and beautiful. And so I couldn't help but laugh at the fact that even though this golfer – who had never taken a formal lesson in his life – had one of the strangest looking golf swings you're likely to come across, he was also the longest and most consistent hitter in his group of golfing buddies.

Often when I'm introduced into a conversation with people I've never met before and they ask me what it is I do for a living, their initial response is to say how lucky I am to be doing something that I love. This is often then followed up by a confession that they would love to either learn or find the time to better their golf game.

But on one particular evening, at a dinner party in south London, I was introduced to someone whose reply was a little different. Quite proud of his sheer lack of sporting skill and potential, this man admitted he had never shown much interest in learning to play any sports, let alone golf. He reflected on the amount of time and money his friends had spent on golf lessons over the years, but still complained they were rubbish on the course.

Finding an unlikely ally to my approach to the game, I heartily agreed with him, and launched into a bit of a monologue about why the golf course is ultimately where the game is learnt and played. I think golfers should be encouraged to get out there and experience the real thing as early as possible rather than spend multiple lessons at the driving range.

In the past this would have been the default for most aspiring players. Most beginners played on the course before ever considering lessons, as there weren't as many teaching professionals and driving ranges as there are today. But as the golfing industry around teaching has grown, far more beginners have adopted the reverse of the past and learnt the technique of the swing first and play later – if at all! I guess, for most people now, the thought of actually heading straight out onto the course before taking any sort of tuition probably seems rather ludicrous and 'risky'.

My own first experience of golf stands as an example here. A friend invited me along to a course to watch him play in the school holidays. We must have been about fifteen. Not expecting to play myself and never having even held a club, let alone taken a swing at a ball, I was a little surprised when on the second tee he handed me his five iron and suggested I have a go. If I remember correctly, I missed it on the first and maybe the second attempt. But when I did eventually hit the ball, to the astonishment of us both, my first ever tee shot sailed beautifully down towards the middle of the fairway.

Exactly how far it went and whether I managed to do it again that day I'm not sure. And there was certainly a huge element of luck involved in my first ever shot flying straight down the fairway. But it didn't matter, because the sensation that I felt from that one incredibly lucky shot out on a real golf course, was enough to make me fall instantly in love with the game. I returned home that day feeling as though I had been seized by this new sport. I excitably retold the story to my parents, persuading them to not only buy me my first set of clubs, which turned out to be a half set of Slazenger's, but also to let me join the same golf club as my friend. Quickly teaming up with some of the other junior members or playing by myself, the game continued to seize me and whenever possible I squandered the whole day happily going round and round the course until it was dark.

The golf club had no professional to offer lessons or proper practice facilities, so the ability to improve outside of playing on the course was limited to a practice net and a small green. On reflection and certainly contrary to what many think about using a practice net, I have to say that the time spent hitting balls into this net was time well spent in improving my swing. I would now urge any new golfer to consider using a net in the early stages of their learning rather than the range. I say this because if you hit balls into a net, it is not possible to see and judge where the ball ends up. Whereas at the driving range, it is all too easy to become obsessed with the length and quality of each shot and so get stuck in a pattern of chastisement for each 'mistake'. With a net, no such focus on results is possible, which meant I had no choice but to learn to 'feel' what a good golf shot was like.

And so, without any idea how to swing a club in a 'textbook' kind of a way or any involvement from a professional, I ended up grooving my own swing. I grew in confidence through positive affirmation from the sensation of the motion rather than from external assurance of whether my swing was 'correct'.

I'm strongly convinced that there was no substitute for the early experience I gained whilst playing out on the course, regardless of how many poor shots I hit or how often I ended up in the woods looking for my ball. In fact, if truth be told, spending so much time playing from off the fairway in my early golfing years helped me learn to enjoy trying to get out of the trouble I found myself in. It also helped me better appreciate the shots that did end up either on the fairway or the green.

So what stops people playing on the course?

I'm going to let you into a secret that many golfers don't want you to know ... most golf courses are not full of brilliant players. In fact, most golfers hit some pretty dreadful shots. I say this not to be mean or to deride the many many golfers who love the game, even with score cards regularly topping 120, but to de-mystify playing on the course and demonstrate that the course is for everyone – no golfer deserves to be out there any more than any other.

I remember one beginner I helped out only last year who was really fearful of the standard of play on the course. She told me she didn't want to step foot on a golf course until she could 'hold her own', which for her meant close to a professional standard of perfection. I did my best to explain that she was already good enough, but I don't think she really believed me. So, I decided to change tactics, and invited her to join me out on my local course for the afternoon, not to play, but just to see for herself what playing the course actually looks like. My objective for the afternoon was to show her the abundance of 'bad' golfers and odd-looking swings that grace every golf course, every day all over the world.

The afternoon got off to a good start – as we made our way to the first tee, we stopped to let a group of four of the club members tee off from the fifth. Luckily for me I knew two of them and was sure at least one of them would help me out with demonstrating the 'diversity' of swings seen on the course. We were not disappointed, although I think the club member was by the words he muttered under his breath. His swing hit the top of the ball, sending it barely 20 yards, whilst another member of the group sliced their ball into the trees to the right.

Calling it a day after the ninth hole, we walked back to the club house for a well-earned refreshment. My client was visibly more relaxed, and we laughed as we reflected on the very many odd-looking swings and shots we had witnessed during our round, including some of my very own. I think the most important thing she took away from that afternoon is that the golfers she saw playing 'badly' were still able to have fun and enjoy the game despite, and sometimes because of, the off-beat shots they made. She witnessed the cama-raderie of searching in vain for a ball in the rough, the cheers when a golfer finally got the ball out of the bunker on their fourth attempt and the joy of the golfer who's ball finally went in on the eighteenth hole after a mare of a round.

There's no doubt that playing on the course can at times be extremely challenging and frustrating for any golfer, and particularly for a beginner, but – and this is a big but – it can also be extremely rewarding and wonderful if you accept that you're just like everybody else out there.

For anyone who might consider taking my advice,

and starting their golf on the course, there are a few key things that I'd suggest taking into account.

Pick your time

The key to playing for the first few times is to try and not put yourself under any sort of unnecessary pressure. Make those first few visits with a friend, either to walk round with you or play themselves, and visit when the course is at its quietest, maybe in the late afternoon or evening when most of the members or regular golfers will be back in the club house or back at home. If you don't fancy beginning on the first hole because its visible from the club house, then don't. Start halfway down the fairway and out of sight, it really doesn't matter. I'd also recommend playing just a few holes to begin with, building up to nine, which may be enough for many golfers, there is no imperative to play the full eighteen, just as a tennis game doesn't always have to run to five sets.

What you need from your first few experiences is to get a feel of what it's like to take a swing on grass, an uneven lie, from the rough and maybe even from a bunker. It's best not to try too hard, concentrate or worry too much about where the ball goes as this can leave you feeling paralysed and lost. It's encouragement, enjoyment and getting a sense of the reality of playing on the course that matters.

Use multiple balls

A big part of the reason that I got better at golf came from the fact that I took most shots not once, but twice, and sometimes multiple times. I'd just throw down another ball either after a poor shot or simply because I wanted to experience a similar shot again from a slightly different position or lie. I remember one example fondly from my early golfing years and is a story that I will often retell to my clients now.

The eighth hole at my local course was a very daunting par-four for me, that required an extremely accurate, long tee shot through what seemed a very narrow tunnel of trees. I found myself nestled in the green side bunker after a misguided four-iron from the fairway. I dug into the sand and managed to loop the ball out and over the green to the bunker on the other side. Not quite what I'd meant to do. With no other golfers playing behind me, I went to my bag and dropped a number of balls into the sand to practice the shot again. I kept going, and something like ten attempts later my ball rose beautifully out of the sand, onto the green and ran straight as a die into the hole. My elation was only matched by the two other balls that also found the hole soon after. Of course, I totally accept that it was a stroke of luck that the balls did indeed go into the hole ... and if truth to be told, I don't think I have ever repeated such a feat again. But the point is that what I did that day was find a style of bunker shot that worked for me. I didn't know what technique I was supposed to use, and my style was not at all what you're 'supposed' to do ... I used the leading edge of the club face rather than the traditionally taught back edge of the club face. But it didn't matter because it worked.

It was this type of self-reflective, trial-and-error style of practice out on the course, without any formal instruction, that taught me to play a bunker shot. More importantly, it offered me a high degree of confidence in my own ability and style. In fact, for a long time after, whenever I approached a bunker shot, I would remember back to that day of the three holed shots and see it as a joyful challenge, and not something that I had to think too much about.

The rather sad thing about this story is that once I started to become more familiar with how the textbooks taught the bunker shot, I tried to adapt my style to be more 'correct'. It rocked my confidence and I have never again captured the same freedom, assurance and control in the bunker that I had years earlier when I knew nothing except how I played the shot myself.

Use just a few clubs

I'd strongly recommend that beginners learn to play the game with just a few clubs in their bag rather than the full fourteen which is permitted. In fact, if I peek into my bag, which is sat right next to me now as I write, I can see my putter, fifty-six-degree wedge, five irons and my new three wood. I very rarely carry a full set as I don't like carrying a heavy bag full of clubs. And I also love the challenge this brings to the game, forcing me to be more imaginative and creative with my shot-making, which by the way has improved both my game and also my enjoyment.

For a beginner, carrying fewer clubs is even more important. Firstly, it's a long walk round a golf course, and lugging a heavy bag with fourteen clubs will only make it feel longer. Fewer clubs also means it's a lot less intimidating and confusing to decide which club to use and means you can become familiar, comfortable and consistent with the swinging of each club far quicker than with a full set.

Even if a beginner does decide to carry the full set, the chances of actually using them all are fairly slim. A classic example of this happened when I took a very enthusiastic beginner client of mine out onto the course for the first time. As we were stood chatting on the first tee I had to chuckle a little as I noticed he was flaunting a brand-new set of clubs, which he had literally bought ten minutes earlier from the pro shop. The bag consisted of three wedges, seven irons, two hybrids, a three wood, driver and a putter. Not only did he have fifteen clubs, one more than the rules of golf say you're allowed, but they still had their plastic wrappers on. By the end of our round he was puffing from the weight of carrying so many clubs round the course and had only unwrapped five of them. To cut a long story short, it must have been about six months later that we arranged to meet for another on-course lesson. As we stood on the first tee, I noticed that half the clubs still had their wrappers on, so I assumed when I asked him that he hadn't played since our last game. *Oh yes*, he replied, *Ever since that very first lesson I've been playing almost every week now.* That did make me a laugh a little.

Don't keep a score

My wife is very competitive. She has a beautiful, natural swing, but doesn't play golf very often, so has the game you'd expect of an occasional golfer – brilliant at times, but with a lot of random mis-hits and unintentional shots. But despite this, she absolutely insists on keeping score whenever we're out on the golf course. This means that rather inevitably each round ends with disappointment, as her score card is never going to reflect her expectations. I think it's a real shame, and here make a public plea for her to change her focus. Because actually, her score card result obscures the fantastic moments present in each round when she makes a brilliant tee shot onto the fairway, or beats me with her chip from off the green or holes a 10ft putt. These moments are what make up the quality of her round, not her score card mired with random shots into the rough, lost balls and mis-hits.

So I always advise my beginner clients or occasional

golfers not to record or worry about their score. It's immaterial in the beginning and like in the case of my wife can sap confidence early in the learning process.

Ignore the rules

As long as you follow simple golfing etiquette, you mustn't be scared to ignore the rules ... Ignore the rules, I hear you shudder. Well of course there is a time and place to understand and follow some of the rules of golf. They are there for a reason and sometimes they can actually be a benefit to your game rather than making it harder. But, until the time you decide you're ready to join a club and start playing competitions – which for many won't happen for a while, if ever – I'm convinced that worrying about following the strict rules of golf will just be a hindrance. No one is going to throw you off the course because your club touches the sand before you play your shot. No one is going to care if you decide to tee the ball up on the fairway to be kind to yourself whilst you're learning your swing. Or as a friend of mine once announced to me some years ago as he politely kicked his ball back onto the fairway, *I don't pay my membership fees to play from behind trees.* And if the going gets tough, and you've really had enough of a hole, there's no law that prohibits picking the ball up and then re-dropping it further on or on the next hole.

And this point about rules doesn't just apply to beginners, I think all golfers could do with relaxing and flaunting the rules a little at times. Don't get me wrong, as I just mentioned there's a time and place for rules, and when I was aspiring to be a professional I loved them. I cared about every shot I played, always striving to improve my handicap and game. I played many rounds not taking mulligans, counting each and every shot and recording my results and stats. But now that I'm playing nearly all my golf purely for the fun of it, I'm enjoying the fact that I can now play without the added pressure of doing everything strictly by the book. I must admit that when I'm playing with my wife or certain friends, there isn't a round when we don't have at least one cheeky 'celebrity drop' or mulligan as it's more commonly known. And boy does that make the game far more enjoyable and easier.

And it's not only golf that I think benefits from a bit of relaxing of the traditional rules ... I think you can increase your enjoyment of most sports by not sweating the small stuff and playing with more freedom.

Whenever I get the chance, which is not as frequently as I'd like, I have a game of tennis. Playing with one particular friend who is pretty much at the same level as me in terms of experience and ability, we came to the conclusion that the serve itself was both infuriating and detracting from our overall experience. And so, after a little debating, we ended up dropping the more traditional serve and replacing it with a far simpler under arm version, the only requirement being to get the ball over the net. Not satisfied with just the one adjustment, we also made it a rule that the ball and the point was not 'live' until it had crossed the net four times. What resulted from these slight breaches of the rules was not only an immediate and drastic improvement in our number of rallies, but also a dramatic improvement to our technique as we were now getting to play far more shots per rally than previously possible.

Be kind to yourself

All of the ideas above come from the same foundation, which is to be kind to yourself. For most people, golf is a game played for fun and enjoyment, so anything you can do to decrease your stress, and feel more relaxed and 'groovy' on the course is good by me. I'm not saying for a second that there won't be frustrating, difficult and disappointing times playing golf – there are for all of us. But if you can work hard to be kind to yourself, to forgive yourself for mistakes and to congratulate the small victories, then you're far more likely to persist. And it's worth remembering that these frustrations and difficulties would be present even on the driving range, if not more so ... I've seen many a golfer fuelled by frustration, hitting balls over and over again to try and rectify an error, becoming more and more irate as the balls continue not to conform. In contrast, on the course between each shot you have a chance for space. As you walk to your ball, you can bring your mind back to the bigger picture, look at your surroundings, or share a joke with a friend, thus relieving the tension and approaching the next shot on better terms. And when you hit a good one, it's far more likely to get ingrained in your memory than on the range, where each shot blends with the others.

So please remember to be kind, to encourage yourself rather than to punish and chastise. The more relaxed and happier you feel, the more likely you will be to play, forming a virtuous circle of improvement and enjoyment.

So get out there, and get a real taste of what this beautiful game called golf really means. Golf isn't about hitting hundreds of balls from a mat on the driving range. It's not about learning to hit perfectly straight with a seven iron or worrying about the rules. It's about looking out at the quiet beauty of a course covered in mist as you take your first shot; it's about feeling the sun on your back as you walk down the fairway with a good friend; it's about negotiating dog legs, figuring out how to hit a shot from under a tree, or in the middle of a bush; and it's the euphoria of hearing the noise of the ball as its drops into the hole. These are all just as much a part of the game as the swing itself, and quite frankly it's what brings the game to life.

CHAPTER FOUR

What Descartes Taught Me

Keeping it simple

In 2012 a very good friend of mine sadly passed away. Some of my fondest memories of Alex are times spent round his flat. I remember our long chats about life, golf, photography and tennis, I remember the epic (and lucrative) putting competitions we had in his large lounge, but most of all I remember the cooking. Alex was a wonderful cook and professional chef, and as a complete novice in the kitchen – probably a twenty-one handicapper in golfing terms – I used to love hanging around in his kitchen, feasting on the sights and smells and occasional tastes of the many dishes he would effortlessly conjure up. I remember one particular occasion when I asked him to help me cook a meal for a new girlfriend I was hoping to impress. He dismissed out of hand the flamboyant dishes I found in a fancy cook book, making it quite clear that attempting to follow these complex recipes as a novice was more likely to end in disaster and a trip to McDonalds than tasting or looking like the pictures in my recipe book. Instead he advised that I use a few good quality ingredients and keep it really simple. His reasoning was that the key to cooking as a beginner was to do simple things well and leave the technical stuff to the professionals. In the end we agreed on a simple pasta dish with prawns and chilli, followed by an easy chocolate mousse. I'm pleased to report that it went down rather well ... and my girlfriend is now my wife.

Golf is not a religion, and yet the teaching of the game can feel like it is at times. The almost zealous adherence to step-by-step techniques and principles can strip us of our ability to think for ourselves, placing us at the mercy of golf professionals and, in fact, anyone with an opinion.

As I recall in the chapter above, in my early learning of the game, I was blissfully unaware of what I 'should' be doing and how, and simply developed a style that worked for me. That began to change as I improved and started playing in more competitions. For the first time, other golfers were witnessing my game, and even though my handicap was quickly diminishing, there still seemed to be a collective sense that I needed to be 'taken in hand'. Suddenly I had a collection of golfers, mostly older men, offering me heartfelt advice and guidance on how to improve. Of course, I was immensely grateful for the advice. I felt that I had missed out on the benefit of tuition and was scared that I somehow wasn't playing the game 'correctly'. Like so many golfers past and present, I fell into the trap of thinking that I needed to make big changes to my game to progress. So, I took on all the advice and, as you would expect, I was captivated and excited by the promise of improvement. The advice sounded so clever, so scientific, so guaranteed to work, that I tried each and every new idea, from a different grip to a different swing.

And why not? When you're learning something new it's not easy to be brave enough to ignore or challenge advice, even if it doesn't really fit for us and doesn't produce the effect promised. It can seem almost rude or ungrateful to reject the support of those that we trust and who seem more experienced than us. And in placing our game in the hands of others, there's also a sense of security – we no longer have to think for ourselves because others have the 'magic' answers, the right way to learn. In some particular circumstances I think the power of the so-called 'expert' to offer advice can be exploitative, even if it is given benignly.

Slowly my natural, fluent style became confused and

fractured by the many pieces of advice swirling round my head. Seeds of doubt about my ability and skill were sown, first my confidence decreased and then my game deteriorated. It was many years before I re-found my natural style and re-discovered my early simple love of the game.

And it's not just people like me who aspire to play professionally who can find themselves in this situation. For anyone deciding to play golf these days, the first step is nearly always golf lessons. And golf lessons in the UK today almost certainly mean meeting with an expert who will impart a whole load of advice, diagnostics and discussions, which is likely to leave the student dizzy with the array of things on which to focus, the errors needing rectifying, the deficits needing work. It's my experience that this traditional style of teaching reinforces the idea that golf is technical and that golf is difficult, and makes the initial learning or improving process frustrating and joyless.

And what's more, those that do 'get through' this teaching system often end up reliant on the pro to play the game, rather than themselves. This might be ok whilst lessons continue, but out on the course, when you need to draw on your own feel and intuition to play each shot, the reliance on tuition is a huge disadvantage.

It seems like such a dreadful shame to me that tuition so often dampens enthusiasm and excitement for the game rather than fanning it, that playing on the course can seem a more distant prospect after six lessons than it was in the first, and that as a result, many of those ready and eager to learn end lessons with the conclusion that golf isn't for them.

Something is going very wrong here! In many other sports, from tennis to football, complete beginners just get on and give it a go. Yes, there are coaches and pros to help, but tuition doesn't seem to dominate in the same way it does in golf, particularly in the beginning before any essence of the game is formed. Personally, I think it's time to step back from the oppressive influence of some forms of tuition and look with fresh eyes at the learning process.

When I provide tuition, I try to stress to my clients' the importance of finding their own game, and encourage them to get out there and learn on the course, to learn through observation – all ways to learn and improve without the assistance of someone like me! But the reality is still that many people want to start their learning journey or return to learning with the support of tuition, either through a golf pro, books or the internet. So, with this in mind, I offer the following ideas to find a teacher that works for you.

Keep it simple

I've worked with many different people in my coaching career, and what I've learnt very clearly is that there is no one right way to teach – because there is no one way to learn. Some of my clients like to learn through watching, others by doing. Some like to understand the theory, others more the 'feel'. But the one thing that I'd say is consistent for all my clients is the importance of keeping it simple. No one can learn when they are bombarded with too much information, particularly if this is not in the right format for them. So, first of all make sure the format of teaching you use is suited to you – this may mean learning through reading a book, learning through copying a swing or learning through discussion with a golf pro. Next, make sure that the approach to learning is not too generic or too technique driven. If the advice given applies to anyone learning to play golf, rather than being tailored to you, it's unlikely to be effective. And finally, and most importantly, check that's it's not too complicated ... Golf is not a complicated game to learn and so any tuition that makes it so should be avoided.

Keep it consistent

What do Serena and Venus Williams, Rafael Nadel, Andy Murray, Jim Furyk, Justin Thomas and Tiger Woods have in common? They were all coached by a single person in the key early stages of their career. There's something about this dedicated, consistent and trusting presence that allowed these sports professionals to flourish, being able to block out all the noise, all the hysteria, and just focus in on developing their own game.

And I think there's an important lesson here for any learning, and particularly for golf. If we draw on multiple sources, chopping and changing the approach to learning that we take, then the result can be very muddled. Instead, I always advise people who want to take golf lessons to take the time to find a golf pro that they get along with, and whose approach fits for them – check that you can work together first. And once you're clear, I advise that you commit to that style of learning and to that teacher. It's tempting to change approach or pro when things aren't going well, but learning is never a clear upward trajectory, and if you can commit and trust in your teacher through the ups and downs, you're likely to come out the other side clearer and more self-reliant than entering a spiral of constantly changing your technique or your teacher.

And the same thing applies to well-meaning advice from friends and family too. A few years ago now, I had the pleasure of coaching two young women who wanted to learn golf to join their husbands on the course. The tuition had gone well, they'd both found their natural, unconscious swing, and then we'd focused in on two simple principles – using the lower body to help facilitate the swing and keeping balanced. In no time, they were ready for their first foray onto the course. Unfortunately, their report afterwards was less than glowing! They'd started off really well, keeping it simple, remembering the feel of the swing, and had taken my advice to try not to worry too much where their balls were ending up. So far so good, but then, perhaps predictably, they told me how their husbands started chipping it. *Try holding the club a bit lower. Don't forget to keep your head still. Now where you went wrong there was …* By the ninth hole, my two budding golfers were fed up, frustrated and barely on speaking terms with their well-meaning spouses.

They returned to our next lesson disheartened. The remedy was simple, I said, either their husbands agreed to keep quiet and allow them to find and groove their own game, or their husbands would be banned from the course. I imagine I was none too popular in the households of these clients, but no matter, it worked, and having checked in regularly with these two clients over the years, I can report that they are now offering their husbands the advice.

Don't throw the baby out with the bath water

The final point I want to make about using tuition refers to our human tendency to discard everything we know at the first sign of a new idea. We see it in national politics all the time where new candidates claim to have the answer we've all been waiting for and that everything the other party has done is rubbish. In fact, reality is always a bit greyer than these black and white extremes suggest. And so with golf ... a classic example of this was back in the day when I was an assistant professional learning my trade. I taught Ted, one of the club members, who I think at the time was a sixteen-handicap golfer and had been playing the game for about twenty years. Managing to avoid tuition completely until about six months prior to our first meeting, he had decided to take a few lessons in the hope of squeezing a little bit more distance out of his drives. Unfortunately, the opposite happened and what he actually ended up with was a complete swing change and a slice.

By the time he saw me, Ted was really cross and pretty disillusioned by golf tuition all round, cautioning me before we started not to *ruin his game any further*. So, instead of further changes, I suggested that he try and put aside what he had recently been taught and the new swing he was attempting to develop and invited him to try and recreate his swing of old. With twenty years' worth of swinging the same way in the bank, it didn't take him that long to re-capture the feeling that was his old swing.

Ok, his drives were only landing on average between 180 and 200 yards, but he was hitting the ball much more consistently into the middle portion of the fairway. More importantly, he now seemed much happier. You could almost see the frustration lift from his shoulders as he once more saw his trusty and familiar shot return with his driver.

Watching him swing the club as he had done for most of his golfing life, the first thing that I noticed was that his lower body was almost completely static throughout the swing. This is pretty unusual – without the lower body getting behind the swing, the amount of power generated from the shot is limited. I now understood why he'd been seeing a shortening of his drive in recent years. He was generating all his power through his arms and the twist of his upper body, and that power was now being diminished by age and less flexibility.

I could see how tempting it would be to try and change this, to completely restructure his swing around the power of his lower body. But trying to change the whole way he approached the swing, after twenty years in the game, that's like asking you to change the way you walk or run, practically impossible. Of course you can do it, Tiger Woods took years out of his career to completely restructure his swing ... but Ted didn't want to be Tiger Woods. He just wanted to get his ball down the fairway.

So, swallowing my wish to intervene, I concluded that actually the best course of action was no action. I told him that I thought his swing worked very well for him, and any changes that I could suggest would be really disruptive to his game. I recommended that we end the lesson right there and told him that I thought it best for him to just go back to being the master of his old style and habit. If he really wanted to regain the distance he'd lost over the past few years, I said don't worry about more lessons, just go home and do a few stretches every night. Bestowing me a wry looking smile, he kindly thanked me for reassuring him that his game was better off left alone and departed – perhaps he wasn't going to have the longest drive, but it was a swing he could trust in.

And that's the key really, if you decide to look for tuition to support an aspect of your game, be really clear with the pro what your aim is. If you don't want a complete overhaul of your game, say so! And if the pro does suggest radical change, ask the simple question – is that really necessary? If it doesn't feel right for you, then it probably isn't. So trust in how it feels to you, and what works for you, because ultimately there is no right or wrong way to play this game.

A few years ago now, I got rather into philosophy, and had a go at reading some of the seminal texts, including Rene Descartes . . . I admit, a lot of it went over my head, but there were a few lines that really struck me:

Buildings undertaken and completed by a single architect are usually more beautiful and better ordered than those that several architects have tried to put into shape, making use of old walls which were built for different purposes.

This makes a lot of sense to me, and I think sums up my approach to learning golf: believe in yourself, keep it simple and don't get too many people involved! Perhaps not as profoundly put as Descartes, but you catch my meaning.

CHAPTER FIVE

A Lesson from the Past

The importance of observational learning

'... *a little boy was following Stewart solemnly about the
East Lake course, never minding in the least that the
imperturbable Scot paid him not the slightest attention, but
watching... watching... watching.*'

O B Keeler, The Bobby Jones Story, 1953*

---

* That little boy was Bobby Jones, who went on to become one of the
greatest players of his time, from 1923 to 1930 capturing an amazing 62
percent of all the national championships he entered, including winning
five out of eight US Amateurs and winning the Open Championships
seven times. In 1926, Jones became the first player ever to capture the
'Double', winning the US and British Open Championships in the same
year.

Jones is famed for never having had a golf lesson in his life, learning
entirely by observing other players and practicing on the course.

Around three years ago now, my wife and I decided to take our one-year-old son to Normandy in France. It was where we had spent a few days on our honeymoon and has remained one of our favourite places.

Now for those of you who have children, I'm sure you'll know the perils of trying to plan a long journey around a sleeping baby, and so in the interest of everybody concerned we decided to split the journey up, stopping near Dieppe. We arranged to stay at a beautiful house hidden deep in the forest, which we only found by sheer luck after I printed out the directions in French. Several hours later than expected, after several tense conversations about whether *gauche* was left or right, we arrived and unpacked the military number of boxes that seem to inevitably come with travelling with a one-year-old.

With our little boy soundly asleep, we were very kindly invited to have dinner with the owners and a few of their friends. Enjoying the evening and the company of the other guests, it was about midway through the night when the conversation turned to what we did for a living, and I said I was a golf pro. Our host, Alain, beamed at me. *No, but this is perfect. You are exactly what I need!* he cried. I could have sworn that his wife rolled her eyes slightly, but it may have been a trick of the light. I said that I'd be happy to help, and we arranged an impromptu golf lesson for the next day.

One of the advantages of having a one-year-old is that most mornings you get to see the sun rise, and the next day was no exception. My son woke in high spirits a little after 6am. Wandering out with him in my arms to the garden I was surprised to see our host up bright and early, dragging an extremely dusty set of golf clubs onto the back lawn. He greeted me with an enthusiasm I found hard to reciprocate at that time in the morning and started to dust off each of his clubs. Later in the morning, with my son fed and crawling happily around the garden with my wife, I sat down with Alain to understand more about what he wanted my help with. He told me that he had retired a few years ago and was looking for a new challenge. He'd played rugby and skied and been active all his life but had not until recently tried his hand at golf. The trouble was, his nearest golf club and driving range were about thirty kilometres away. Happy to make the journey to actually play a round of golf, the thought of driving this distance just for a regular lesson and practice seemed a bit much to him. And so he'd tried to teach himself, using his large back garden and the orchard beyond as his driving range, but after a few months had given up, so frustrated was he with his lack of progress. He told me he'd seriously considered binning his clubs, but given that I was here, he'd like to at least get my opinion on what was going wrong.

I suggested that I watch him hit a few balls. *Of course*, he said, and picked up his club. The transformation that took place when he stood over the ball was striking, gone was my relaxed and genial host – his arms were stiff, his back rigid with his fingers gripping the club for dear life. He looked extremely uncomfortable, which was only intensified as he swung the club in what looked like a series of jerky movements rather than one flowing motion.

Unfortunately, this isn't the first time that I've watched a perfectly agile, confident, coordinated adult change so completely when stood over the golf ball. And in my experience, the most common culprit for such paralysis is being taught golf through the dissection of the swing. So, I wasn't at all surprised when he told me that he'd learnt his 'technique' from a series of step-by-step video lessons on the internet, which had shown him how to do everything from grip the club to follow through. The problem though, he told me, was that he was still worrying about his grip from lesson one, keeping his back straight from lesson two, making sure his left arm was straight in lesson three, breaking his wrists in lesson four, trying to swing slower in lesson five, and any number of other things that he couldn't quite remember in lessons six and seven.

No wonder he was struggling. The tendency to dissect and teach each individual part of the swing as a separate component is rife in golf tuition both online and in person. The problem is, how on earth is a beginner supposed to piece together all these separate bits to create anything even closely resembling a natural and consistent swing!

I've said it before, but I'll say it again … we are not machines, we're not designed with a simple input and output processing system. If we were then maybe it would be possible to 'download' the different parts of a professional's perfect swing, and synthetically piece them together into a collection of individually perfect segments that could then be replicated time and time again. But we're not that simple, thank goodness!

Take as comparison the act of walking, an action my son was practicing at the time. You don't learn to walk by learning the different segments of the movement – it would be ludicrous to practice each part as a separate entity – and similarly with the swing, the whole is greater than the sum of the parts. This is not to say that down the line, when the basics are mastered, there isn't merit in understanding what each solitary part of the swing is doing, but to teach each bit as if it was a thing in its own right often ends up with problems like those experienced by my host.

When I witness learners as confused as Alain, I think it's important to spend time clearing that confusion before trying to teach anything else. So, we sat in his beautiful garden and I helped him to understand that it was not necessarily him that had failed to understand the swing, and not been able to hit the ball, but that the method of tuition he had chosen had let him down. Alain could see very quickly the problem that had been created and cursed freely the videos that he had come to rely on, seeing now that they had hindered rather than supported his learning. *So how do I start again?* I was very aware that Alain would not be able to regularly get to a course for lessons or practice, so suggesting a more interactive style of learning would not be effective. And I'm also completely in support of the kind of observational learning you can do through the internet and TV to learn the basics of golf, just not when it involves over technical instruction. So, I suggested that he should change what he watches rather than how he learns.

Even though research has consistently shown the benefit of observational learning, I think a lot of golfers think of watching as a way of learning as a bit lame and ineffective. In fact, sports psychologists Barbi Law and Craig Hall in a 2009 study found that the older the golfer, the less likely they were to use observational learning to improve their game. But I think this is dismissing a potentially important form of learning. We've only got to remember back to childhood to recognise the incredible power of observation. From talking to walking to learning to ride a bike, the main way in which children learn new skills is through watching others and then trying it out for themselves. Observing is crucial for development and is at the bedrock of most sports.

I'd say that most children have watched football, either in the park or on the TV, or watched an older sibling score goals in the garden before the age of three. Tennis courts often sit at the centre of public parks, and Wimbledon is widely watched on TV, the same for cricket, cycling, and swimming – they're part and parcel of our cultural upbringing. And this is where it's a bit different for golf. Courses are often tucked away up private driveways, golfing ranges housed in dark buildings, and golf on TV is only in a minority of households. So, most children are not exposed to golf in the same way they are with other sports from an early age. Instead, many people, like Alain, come to golf much later, without any latent knowledge of what to do, and without the same childlike curiosity and thirst for learning that we once took for granted.

But that doesn't mean that we can't apply the same principles of watching as a form of learning in adulthood. And if this is a style of learning that appeals to you, either out of necessity like Alain, or purely from preference, then there are few key principles that I'd suggest to ensure you watch the 'right' things rather than the 'wrong' things.

Chose a player from the past to study

This may sound obvious, but a great way to get started or return to golf is to watch it! Whether you chose to watch a classic Ryder cup match from the past, or a contemporary tournament happening live, watching these elite professionals drive, play from the fairway, the rough, the bunker and putt will expose you to many examples of different golf swings, shots and styles. Don't worry too much about 'learning' at this stage, just watch with interest, and allow your mind to absorb the different ways in which the players bodies move with each shot.

Next, I'd advise focusing in on one player to follow a bit more closely. It normally makes most sense to choose a player who is close to you in build, so that there is a more commonality in how your bodies are likely to move.

So, for me, having a slimmer, shorter build, I like to model my game on golfers like Rickie Fowler or Rory Mcilroy. If you're taller or more heavily built, you might have more in common with someone like Dustin Johnson, Tiger Woods or Brooks Koepka. And the same applies to female golfers such as Lexi Thompson, Park Sung-Hyun or Georgia Hall.

When looking for a player to follow, an obvious choice might be a contemporary hero like the golfers above and I certainly find it awe inspiring to watch their games in detail. But actually, if the goal is to learn from observing a player's swing, often a better choice is a player from the past such as Nicklaus, Watson, Couples, Ballesteros, Webb, Wright or Sorenstam

Now there is nothing fundamentally different about watching a past player. In fact, there is remarkable consistency across time and golfer in the essential movement of the body during the swing. But the execution of the swing in the hands of the elite athletes who play today is far harder to model than those of the past. I say this because the majority of contemporary elite golfers are like racehorses – every element of their health and wellbeing is monitored and controlled, from what they eat and drink to tailored exercise regimes. This means that their bodies are finely tuned, incredibly flexible and muscular, allowing them to achieve a level of technique that is far beyond what most amateur players can aspire to. In other words, no matter how carefully you watch the body and the swing of someone like Mcilroy or Woods, it's very unlikely you'll be able to model your own body and swing exactly on theirs.

By praising today's golfers, I don't mean to cast aspersions on the past, and it's a question for another time to ask whether these changes have made the modern golfer any better or more consistent. Classic golfers like Nicklaus, Seve, Watson, Sorenstam, Wright and Webb were supremely talented golfers. Their swings were just as beautiful, impressive and efficient and they've collectively won multiple major championships. But they are also more relatable – there was far less focus on the body as a perfectly well-oiled machine in their heyday, so players were slightly less flexible, often less fit and were effectively ordinary people with extraordinary talent.

Watch the body, not the swing

Ok, so you've chosen a player to watch in a bit more detail. Next, I'd suggest finding some good footage of them swinging the club and watching this a number of times over. For many players there will be edited footage of their swing available on YouTube, normally with a commentary on what they're doing at each point. I'd strongly advise you to mute the commentary so that you can focus on what you notice and take from the players movement, rather than an analysis provided by an expert, which is very likely to be overcomplicated and technical.

As you watch the player swing, the key is to focus your attention on what the player's body is doing at each point, rather than on what their club is doing. It's tempting to watch the club and try and replicate where it is – in fact, much golf instruction is based on mimicking the exact position of a pro's club at different points in the swing, from the angle it reaches at the peak of the backswing to the angle at the point of impact. But I think that this focus is genuinely a red herring. It is a player's body movement that is facilitating the swing. The club just responds to that movement, or comes along for the ride – so if you like, the body's movement is the cause and the resulting swing of the club is the effect. I think it makes far more sense to focus on understanding the cause than dissecting the effect, particularly in the early stages of learning.

Inspiration rather than replication

Now it's important to be clear about the point of this kind of learning. Children use observation to inspire their own efforts, and the same applies to adults. The idea is to tap into the essence of the body's movement, to get a real sense of what the body is doing throughout. I'd suggest watching for a while, and then trying out the movement yourself, see how the body feels, then watch some more, and try it again.

If you took a camera and filmed yourself (which by the way I wouldn't recommend that you do) it's very unlikely that your movement would be an exact replication of the golfer that you're watching. But that doesn't matter, you're not trying to 'copy' the swing, like Bobby Jones, you're just trying to take inspiration to develop your own swing

Before we finish this chapter, I want to return briefly to my host Alain and that summer day in his beautiful garden three years ago. After we'd discussed the perils of breaking down the swing, and Alain had let go of some of his frustrations over his false starts at learning golf, we opened his laptop and looked together at the swings of different golfers. Alain decided on Ballesteros as a golfer that he wanted to learn from as he has a similar build, and incidentally a similar temperament.

We watched his swing many times over, focusing in on the rhythm of Seve's swing and the movement of his body. A couple of espressos and the most divine pain au chocolat later, and Alain was animated, grinning widely. *Yes I see, I see,* he said as he once again took up his club and started channelling Seve's swing – the effect was immediate, the tension had lifted, there was a freedom to his movement that hadn't been there before. His wife came down the garden and caught sight of one of the balls sailing sweetly into the apple orchard, she nodded her head to me with a small smile. *You see, Alain, it is not that difficult after all.*

CHAPTER SIX

An Old School Roller Coaster

Some thoughts on the swing

The Roller Coaster

I step into the car, a stomach flutter, a thought of regret. The bar comes down with a thud.

The climb starts its way creaking and climbing bemoaning our fates 'I want to get off!' my whole being screams.

Over the hill we go with a crack and a whoosh, accelerating, speeding, sliding, slipping and rushing clattering and clunking and then rest.

Tick – tick – tick – The climb starts again, a heart flutter and a whistle, and in one breath we dive into the curve – whirling, whipping, winding and back down.

The wheels start grinding and turning, a gasp and brake. We stop. It's over – and back into line.

By Anon

I'm not sure I've ever met a client who wanted to learn golf who didn't want to start with the swing. The swing is to golf like breathing is to living – so utterly fundamental and central that it can be easy to think that they are equivalent, in other words that the swing is golf and vice versa. The amount of thinking, writing, commentary and technology devoted to the under-standing and execution of the swing is so vast that you'd think there was something magical, something otherworldly, about this simple action. Amateur golfers have devoted huge amounts of time, energy and money in an attempt to master this mythical being, and a whole industry has been colonised to cater for these devotees.

And yet, the golf swing is a simple thing, a back and forth continuous motion in which the ball is struck and propelled forward – if you're lucky. But such is the hysteria around the swing that golfers, like Alain, can get themselves into an awful confusion and end up not being able to perform a movement that is actually quite simple. I'm very aware in my teaching that if a golfer fails to achieve confidence in their swing early on, it's very likely to have a negative effect on their future golfing abilities, in some cases causing golfers to give up well before they have the opportunity to realise any potential they have for the game. I think the antidote to this hysteria is simplicity, and that there are three things to be said about the swing which are truly helpful and within the control of any golfer to take on board. So here they are.

Let it swing

The first is to understand that the aim of the swing is not to hit the ball, but to swing the club in a free-flowing continuous motion. This applies to all swings, whether we're talking about a short chip or a full-blooded drive. To explain a bit better what I mean, I'd like you to visualise a roller coaster, preferably an old school one like the one by the pier in Hastings Old Town. After the initial settling down of the children and parents in their carriages, this beast of a coaster pulls away, drawing the carriages smoothly up and up the steep slope right to the top ... there's a moment of calm as the top carriage tips over the zenith, before gravity's pull takes hold and the carriages begin their journey down, gradually gaining more and more speed till it hits the flat track in a flurry of screams.

Ok, so there's usually less screaming in golf, but you get the idea ... the roller coaster exactly captures the pulling up of the back swing, the brief sensation of stillness at the top before the forwards swing begins, smoothly gathering momentum until it reaches maximum speed as it makes contact with the ball. It's a beautiful fluid motion to watch, and one which, like the roller coaster, is best thought of and felt as one ride rather than as a series of different rides. And like the roller coaster it requires the golfer to respect the natural flow and rhythm of the swing, rather than to 'force' or 'control' the pace or its path.

It's that respect for the swing's natural flow, particularly at the point of transition, which is often a very tricky part for golfers. I've witnessed this in very many of my clients, and one who particularly stands out is David, a powerfully built man in his forties who works in the City of London. He'd taken up golf because a big part of his job was entertaining clients, which meant playing golf and fancy dinners at some of the smartest clubs in the South East. This is a classic situation where a round of golf can become far more than walking around trying to get a small ball into a small hole.

The way David described his 'business golf' to me was of a delicate but deliberate display of power and strength, bravery and nerve, whilst all the time having to maintain an outward appearance of laid back fun and friendly small talk. Given these strong under-currents, it was not surprising that David found himself tense and anxious on the golf course, desperate to play a decent round and not risk showing himself or his firm up.

Now as an aside, I'm not much in favour of golf as a vehicle for business. It's a game and it's supposed to be fun, and mixing business and pleasure is for my money not a great idea. But there we are, this has been a function of golf for a very long time, and I imagine my more peaceful, relaxed suggestions will not work for everyone!

But back to David, the pressure seemed to be palpable as he stood over his ball at the beginning of our lesson. He drew his club up fluently, but before it even had space to breathe at the top of his swing, he brought his arms down violently, forcing the club into its descent before it was ready and powering down to smash the ball with a ferocity that showed just how hard David was trying. The ball cruelly sliced off to the right – all that power, effort and energy had come to nil.

David's next shot managed to get 140 yards down the fairway, but the next hooked sharply off to the left, and he stopped, took a deep breath and turned to me with a look of intense frustration. He explained that this type of inconsistency was often his fate on the golf course and that his colleagues loved to point out that his swing was too fast. He'd tried to slow it down, he told me, but how was he going to get any power if he wasn't bringing his club down with some force? I could see the tension lining his face, and wondered what he'd make of my next remarks, but ploughed on regardless.

I told him that the problem wasn't necessarily about the speed of his club – speed is an essential part of all successful golf shots, short or long – but the fact that he was desperately trying to hit the ball rather than swing the club. It's completely understandable, I went on, that when we get to that transition point at the top of the back swing our natural instinct is to try and hit the ball. But it's this attempt to hit at the ball before the swing has had its time to breathe that introduces huge room for error.

The very small chance of this being consistently successful becomes obvious if you think of the huge distance the club is from the ball at the top of the swing. All the energy and motion introduced by forcing the club down too early to hit the ball makes it incredibly hard to stay on the same axis of motion, making it more than likely to strike the ball in any number of inconsistent and unsatisfactory ways, including a complete miss!

If, on the other hand, I said to David, you let go of the aim being to hit the ball, and instead employ your arms to support the club to swing, you are going with the motion not against it. And just like a roller coaster accelerating to its maximum speed when it reaches the straight, a helpful by product of a free-flowing swing is that it will make contact with the ball at the point of maximum momentum.

David looked at me sceptically. I think he thought for a moment I was taking the mick, so alien to him was the idea that he wasn't trying to hit the ball. But he agreed to try it. I took the ball away to further reduce the temptation and asked him to just swing the club naturally and easily and just notice the feeling in his arms and the motion of his body. To start with the urge to hit was clearly still there at the swing's transition point, and so I suggested he imagine my roller coaster analogy at the top of its ascent, the way it almost teeters on the edge before being pulled back down again. With this image in mind, I encouraged him to respect that very brief moment at the top of his swing and trust in the swing to begin its descent, guided rather than forced by his arms. This really helped, and after about ten swings, I stopped him briefly and replaced the ball at his feet and asked him to swing again. His first swing hit the ball sweetly, sending it a decent 160 yards down the middle of the fairway.

Ok, this may have been a little bit of luck for me, but after just a few more goes with the ball it was clear he was really beginning to get it. His aim had changed, and I could now visibly see the flow of his swing. He wasn't trying nearly so hard to hit the ball, but the consequence of this was that the balls began to fly more consistently and sweetly down the fairway.

Use your body

The second thing that I think is important to understand about the swing is where it gets its consistent power from. Power isn't always related to effort or strength. Yes there are always happy accidents, but trying with all your might to hit the ball – particularly with just the arms – doesn't necessarily give you more power. The longest and most powerful driver of the ball in the world today is Rory McIlroy. He

73

is five foot seven, and although incredibly muscular his physical build is slight, if he doesn't mind me saying so. It's not heft or strength or even effort that creates the power in his golf swing, it's technique. And that technique is all about harnessing the power of the body.

And this doesn't just apply to golf – the arms are the part of the body delivering the movement in many sports, whether it be a punch in boxing, a stroke in tennis or a pull in rowing. But in all sports, without an exception that I can think of, it's the body that facilitates the arms' movement and provides the all important 'oomph'. It's much easier in a dynamic sport like tennis to see this – you only need to capture a still of a match to see the athleticism. I particularly love to watch Federer and see the way his body pivots and twists and jumps and braces seemingly all at once as his racquet makes contact with the ball – it is truly his whole being that effortlessly and beautifully hits each shot.

And so for all of us. With any reactive sport we have no choice but to be in motion both before, during and after we connect with the ball ... but it's not so straightforward with golf. It's an unusual sport in the sense that it is non-reactive – we're not responding, we're initiating the action, and so getting the body involved is not as naturally intuitive as it is if we're already on the run. In fact, for many amateur golfers the movement of the lower body is often just a cosmetic afterthought in order to try and emulate the finish position of the top players!

But the reason the top players end up with their bodies flung forwards and round with their club in the air is not an effect, it is a necessary consequence of using their body to swing the club. You can see this clearly if you study a top golfer – without exception their upper body spirals round like a corkscrew as the swing journeys upwards. After the brief moment of respite at the point of transition the lower body begins to untwist, setting off a seamless set of movements through the rest of the body, releasing pent-up power like a cork from a bottle.

The effect on the swing is to drive its natural momentum forwards, carrying it down and through the ball smoother, swifter, stronger and firmer than the arms alone could produce and thereby creating the power to propel the ball huge distances. That's the theory at least, but for a lot of golfers this focus on the body rather than the arms to create the swing is not intuitive, and involves something of a leap of faith as they trust in their body to lead the swing's downwards motion, allowing the arms and club to follow.

The importance of distance to most golfers was palpably brought home to me the next time I met with David. Gone was the progress from the last lesson. He was once again allowing very little room for his swing to breathe before bringing it down with almighty force, audibly grunting with the effort he was making to slam the ball. I asked him tentatively what was going on … quite quickly aware that I seemed to be in trouble. He replied hotly that our lesson hadn't worked and that he'd given up on it after his last round of golf, which had been an embarrassment. On enquiring why, he told me that although his shots had been straighter than usual, his drives had been short, only 200 yards or so down the fairway.

I asked him to recreate the swing he'd used on the golf course and reluctantly he did so. It was all too clear what had happened, he'd faithfully taken my advice and had let go of the urge to hit from the top of the swing, and instead focused on creating a natural flowing motion supported by his arms. This worked well for the shorter shots and accounted for his increased consistency. But for longer shots we needed David's body to start contributing to drive the swings flow and facilitate that extra distance.

The way to get the distance, I told him, was to keep going with the aim to swing the club, but now imagine driving the forward swing with his lower body rather than his arms. *You want me to swing the club with my body?* he asked incredulously. I realised that I was seriously pushing my luck, and that this poor guy, clearly overworked and stressed by the pressure from the city, was seriously questioning his decision to entrust me with his game. And no wonder, what I was asking him to do is difficult for a lot of golfers, as it's pretty counterintuitive to let go of control and trust the body to lead the swings downwards motion.

Worried I was losing him a little, I decided to take a different tact. David has told me that he'd rowed for his university, and so I asked him which part of his body initiated and drove the pulling of the oars. He seemed rather reluctant to admit that yes, it was his legs that set the motion off and the arms that followed. *Right then*, I said, *it's just the same with golf.* Of course you can swing a club or row a boat with just your arms, but it's bloody hard work, and it's only when you get the rest of the body involved that you can really start to power through the water, or up the fairway.

To David's credit, he pulled back from what I expect was his urge to leave, and took up the club, visualising his lower body powering his next swing. ... To start with, nothing changed, and his primal urge to hit the ball with his arms still fuelled his downward swing, but slowly I could see this changing ... his lower body became more active, his swing more reactive. Asking him to pause, I once again placed a ball beneath his feet, hoping fervently that this was going to work! His first attempt was still a hit, in the not so good sense of the word, but the second, the third and the fourth were swings effortlessly fuelled by the movement of his lower body – the balls started to soar comfortably past the 200-yard mark. The mixture of incredulity, amazement and triumph on David's face is something that I remember to this day. And I'm pleased to say that this lesson was the start of something of a friendship – or at least a healthy professional respect between us. And whenever we meet up for a top-up lesson, I'll just gently remind him: *Use your body, swing don't hit.*

Create a platform

The third and final thing that is important to understand about the swing is the importance of creating a firm foundation, or platform, from which to approach the back swing. Now it might seem a bit strange for this to be the third rather than the first thing to know about the swing, given that chronologically it happens before the other two, but I have my reasons! I want to put the backswing in its rightful place as playing second fiddle to the forward swing.

Despite the acres of discussion and instruction devoted to it, the back swing's sole purpose is to set up the possibility for a consistent transition and forward swing. There's no point spending hours and hours constructing a 'perfect' backswing if you don't understand what facilitates and drives the forward swing – you could still miss the ball.

I'm sorry to be mixing my metaphors, but I was out for a walk in the woods near my home the other day, and it was pretty blustery. I looked up at the beautiful old trees I was walking through, and was struck quite forcibly that this of course was the perfect way to describe the golfing platform. This could perhaps be considered rather a mundane thing to be contemplating, but there we are, an insight into my golf-obsessed inner world. The trees' branches were swaying and rocking wildly in the strong breeze, the whole wood seemed to be moving in response to the wind's force, and yet the trunks remained stable, grounded and solid.

Essentially, that's what I'm suggesting a golfer should try and emulate during the back swing. To stay as grounded as the trunk of a tree doesn't mean remaining stock still though – trees are in constant motion, but it does mean staying balanced and constant with minimal movement of the legs from side to side, minimal movement of the body forwards and backwards, and minimal up or down movement of the upper body.

This was an aspect of the swing that came very naturally to David. His backswing was able to glide soundly up with his body, acting as a solid platform around which the movement could take place. This seemed entirely instinctive to him and was a real strength of his style. But unfortunately, this isn't the case for everyone ... particularly those who have been exposed to certain types of tuition. Too often, I have met with golfers who have spent lessons and lessons working on their club position at different points in their back swing. Trying their hardest to make sure their club is at the right angle and trajectory at each point, often drawing on video footage of the best players to emulate or filming themselves to check their club is in the 'correct' position. And this is such a mistake! Because there is no correct position ... you've only got to watch the best players to see the variety of back swings out there.

What often results from this misplaced focus is a lot of unnecessary movement in the body as it tries its best to create these 'perfect' club positions. The result is instability. Without that solid platform to create the swing, the back swing is mechanically formed, full of tension and crucially is unlikely to set up the right conditions to execute a consistent transition and forward swing.

When a golfer's back swing goes astray, my focus is all about getting back to basics, to the body and to things that are within their physical and emotional control. Instead of studying the back swings of good golfers, I encourage my clients to look at the bodies of good golfers ... Because this is where the consistency in their technique lies. All good golfers possess in common a balanced golfing platform from which their backswings operate. Just like trees have in common a constant strong trunk round which branches uniquely rotate. And so this is what an amateur golfer can begin to cultivate – not the uncontrollable parts of the back swing like how it looks, where the club is, or what angle it takes, but a solid, sturdy, reliable and constant trunk.

Of course, adopting this freer and less mechanical approach to your back swing may well fashion a more unique and less 'text book' looking back swing. But embrace it! It's these idiosyncrasies that will define your swing and create consistency not matched by those striving for perfection. You only need to look and enjoy the swing of Jim Furyk to believe me.

CHAPTER SEVEN

Hanging Upside Down and Other Ways to Find the 'Zen'

Managing the mind on the course

'(Sometimes) you will come face to face with the sudden and shocking realisation that you are completely crazy. Your mind is a shrieking, gibbering madhouse on wheels barreling pell-mell down the hill, utterly out of control and hopeless. No problem. You are not crazier than you were yesterday. It has always been this way and you never noticed.'

Bhante Henepola Gunaratana,
Sri Lankan Theravada Buddhist monk.

Golf can provide a wonderful relief from the stress and strains of the day, a chance for solitude or company, air and sky, beauty, time, space. But just like when you go on holiday, all the potential or foreseen benefits, the zen-like qualities that seem within our grasp, can get rather messed up by the inevitable and sometimes unwanted presence of our endlessly, tirelessly whirring minds.

I tend to find that my mood on any given day is brought onto the course with me, and I don't think I've ever met a client whose wider personality doesn't infiltrate their game in some way. So, if you're having a frustrating day, you're likely to feel frustrated by the game; if you're feeling tense, it's odds on your swing will feel tight; if you're feeling good, the round is likely to go well; if you're generally a calm, relaxed person, I can bet you'll be a chilled golfer; and if you are prone to anger then you're likely to feel the rage on the course too.

It's a shame in a way that we can't leave our big, brilliant minds back in the clubhouse and try on a different outlook for a couple of holes and see what life would be like through a different lens. But unfortunately it's not as simple as that, the stories we tell ourselves about who we are and what we're like tend to get cemented, built up and solidified over time, so that the idea of being something different feels at best difficult, and at worst impossible.

And this isn't only true of the amateur golfer.

Professional sports people are dogged by their minds in much the same manner, perhaps more so because when the pressure mounts and the stakes are higher, this is when our minds are likely to whisper to us the hidden doubts, the long-disguised fears, the terrors that haunt even the strongest, most even tempered of us. It's the mind that squanders a six shot lead, misses a 4 ft putt, finds the water and loses tournaments, not the body, and it's the ability to manage the mind which determines who the top hundred golfers are in the world out of the thousands who are equally talented.

Golfers like Jack Nicolas and Jordan Spieth stand out for me as having the ability to manage and corral their minds, allowing them to channel positivity and confidence as a way of life, seeming to have as much control and poise off the course as they do on it. Then there's a slightly different type of golfer – those who manage to have extreme discipline and focus on the course, but don't seem as able to maintain that steely calmness and mind control off the course, golfers like Woods. Then there's the even rarer kind of sportsperson who seem to have been able to reign in their formerly rioting mind, athletes like Federer, who in his early twenties rewrote the story of who he was and how he would behave in a way that many around him did not know he was capable of doing. In gaining control of his mind, Federer went on to arguably be the best tennis player ever to have walked on a court. It seems to me that the work and expense the modern sports professional puts into getting to know and understand their minds is just as important, if not more important than the work they put into honing their bodies and their sporting techniques.

It's interesting then, that for the vast majority of those I teach, when I raise the idea of looking at the mind, and the part that it might play in their game, I'm often met with at best scepticism and at worst horror, and have been told a number of times to not go there. And I get it, for most of us we play golf to escape the mind, not to confront it. But annoying as this may be, the more we try and get away from it, the harder the mind pushes to have its point of view heard. And for some of us, that point of view can be pretty negative.

Over the years, I've had a good go at taming my own mind. I've seen colleagues and professionals manage their minds with varying degrees of success and I've supported a number of clients in their mission to tame theirs. And in doing so, I've built up quite a good idea of what helps to soothe and calm the mind, and what fires it further. So, here they are, my mind whispering tips.

Looking at life from a different angle

In my time as a golf teacher I've met some amazing people, but perhaps none more so than my former client, and now friend, Frank. Frank is one of the most positive, enthusiastic and can-do people I have ever met. A man in his fifties, he is an extremely successful businessman, investing and crafting investment for a whole host of businesses, from start-ups to multi-nationals. He even helped me out with building a golf app, investing his time, money and boundless energy into the venture, and keeping that enthusiasm despite it not exactly taking the world by storm. I remember he took me and my wife out to dinner to spend the 'profits' – it was a lovely meal, but let's just say that there wasn't much profit left for dessert.

Anyway, I remember some years ago now, soon after we'd first met, he got in contact asking to have a playing lesson with me out on the course. He told me his game had been off for a while, and he needed a bit of a reboot. I was pleased to agree. It's always a pleasure playing with Frank. But that day I remember Frank really was playing appallingly, the balls were pinging everywhere, the putts were going hopelessly by, he was duffing his pitches. It wasn't anything like his usual game.

Now, with a lot of my clients, when they're playing this badly you can really feel it – the bad vibes radiate from them and the game can descend into a dark, stormy and silent affair, with me trying to provide some comfort and solace where I can. But not with Frank. Time and again he was able to laugh at the way he was playing, shake off yet another bad shot to approach the next with a calm and focus, and let go of his frustration to appreciate the beauty of the course. I was amazed. I'd never seen someone maintain such self-composure, and certainly couldn't have managed to do it myself. After the round when we were having a consolatory drink in the club house, I asked him how he did it. *Well*, he said, *I think the key is hanging upside down every morning.* I kid you not, that is what he said to me. I rather coughed into my drink and asked him, not entirely politely, what he was talking about. Frank went on to tell me that for the last ten years he'd been hanging upside down for an hour each morning and meditating, as a way of strengthening his body, his resolve and centring himself for the day. I was fascinated, and hooked. We stayed in that club house for hours with me asking question after question to understand more about him and from him … about his philosophy in life, how to approach each day afresh, how he had come back from bankruptcy and a failed marriage at the age of thirty-five, and how his mental and physical discipline, forged by a hell of a lot of hours upside down, had resulted in an ability to combine his extreme determination and will for success with this ability to accept and move on when things didn't go to plan. And it was this rather wonderful combination of abilities that meant that within a week of that disastrous round, he'd taken the little advice I offered him, regrouped and had re-found his natural rhythm and game.

I'm not sure how possible it is to emanate Frank; he is an unusual and rather brilliant man and I'm not suggesting you strap yourself to some mechanical device that will enable you to hang upside down every morning. But when I hit a series of bad shots and the world is beginning to seem very dark, I like to think of Frank and his ability to laugh it off and let it go. I almost picture him in my situation and think what he might do, and it seems to help my mind to calm down and stop panicking, which makes the bad shots a bit easier to deal with. I think everyone needs a bit of moral support from a Frank equivalent to draw strength and inspiration from. So, whether it's Gandhi, your best mate Steve or your Great Aunt Maude, make sure you can hold someone in mind to give you strength when the going gets tough.

Building better memories

I don't think there's a golfer out there who isn't accompanied onto the golf course by the spectre of past bad shots stored in her mind, ready to be released in the first moment of doubt. It might be the mind begins whispering even on the first hole ... *remember that time you topped it ... hit it straight in that wood ... scored a 9 here*. Or it might lull you into a false sense of security until things get tough, and then drop in a helpful clanger to remind you of past errors. *You always miss shots from this distance ... didn't you go straight over the green last time you were here etc. ...* Perhaps it's only Frank who doesn't have his own personal doom-mongerer sitting on his shoulder, ready and willing to put in their 'oar'.

When I first started playing I hardly ever heard from the doom-mongerer, such was the optimism and naivety of youth. But there came a time, after I'd taken on a whole load of outside advice and 'help', when it really started to affect me ... I couldn't go a single hole without a helpful reminder of my past ineptitude, personal failings, or inability to improve. It got me down, and my game stalled, and to begin with at least I didn't know what to do about it.

It's the same for so many of my clients – the ledger of past errors is so much easier for them to recall than the times it's gone well. Take Steph, a young woman who'd been playing on her local course for about a year. The first time I met her at *Urban Golf*, she was able to give me an incredibly detailed run down of the shots she'd sliced, topped, missed and mishit on her last outing to the course, but on asking her about times it had gone better, we drew a bit of a blank. She told me it was because there were no good shots, but that seemed so unlikely given the way she was hitting them straight down the fairway in our practice lesson.

We agreed to meet at her local course so I could get a

sense of the problems in situ, so to speak. After a nice first drive Steph found her ball in a divot, a little unlucky but that's golf; the course owes you no favours. She instantly recalled a time this had happened before and told me this was just the kind of shot that causes her problems. I encouraged her to forget that for now, and just focus on getting this shot up and away. Perhaps predictably, it was another poor shot, which Steph accepted with a sigh, and a *see what I mean,* before picking up her bag and going to move on. At this point I stopped her. *Hang on a minute there*, I said, *let's try that again.* Looking rather guiltily behind us at the empty fairway to check we weren't holding anyone up, Steph reluctantly put down another ball, with the prediction that it would go the same way as the last. It did, and so I suggested she try again. After about five attempts, without any advice from me, she played two nice shots in a row. *Now we move on,* I said.

On the second hole, Steph again hit a nice tee shot followed by two ok shots, the second of which finished about 5 yards off the green. Once again, the lie was poor, the ball sitting down in the grass. Frustrated by the lie, Steph went on to hit a poor chip which shot across the green and into the bunker. Again, she immediately went towards the bunker to play the next shot and again I stopped her and called her back. It took about five attempts but then she got her eye in and proceeded to hit three or four nice ones in a row.

We continued on round the nine holes in this fashion,

me hoiking her back after each bad shot to replay it until it came out right. By the time we reached the ninth, Steph had hit about eight different types of bad shots but had about sixteen good repeat shots to dilute the memory. It's quite a basic idea, but this is what I found worked brilliantly for my own game when the doom-mongerer began to take up residence on my shoulder. I played a lot by myself, and every time I'd hit a dud shot, I'd drop more balls, and keep playing until I figured it out. That way, rather than sinking under the weight of my mind recalling bad shots, I'd begun to collect new stories to tell myself. And when a doom-mongering thought is countered by a whole host of evidence to the contrary, I find it doesn't take long for it to slink away, beaten by the force of the counter stories.

And so it was with Steph, after a few rounds playing in this way, she'd built up a whole host of positive memories and reported being able to approach her shots with a lot more confidence. Working in IT, she told me that she thought of it as a process a lot like being 'reprogrammed'. Whether you call it telling new stories, reprogramming or whatever, I don't think it matters – the key is to not allow those doom-mongering thoughts to have a free rein.

Let it in, let it be, let it pass

Dominique stood in the sim at *Urban Golf* and proceeded to hit about ten seven-irons carrying an average of 180 yards and finishing within a very acceptable distance of each other. Nice, I thought as he took his driver out, comfortably and consistently carrying his drives 280 yards. He definitely had some talent.

I wondered what such a confident and competent golfer might need from my tuition. *Well* he said with rather a wry laugh, *it might look good right now, but get me in front of a stream, lake, ditch or bunker, and my swing goes to pieces*. He told me how his local course is a particularly watery one, and that without fail he'd plop his ball into the drink at least once every round, sometimes more often, as well as finding nearly every bunker on the course. This was not only ruining his score, racking up a hefty price in replacement golf balls, but also getting him a bit of an unkind reputation with his friends as a gasman, which I gather means someone who can't take the heat.

Fairly common, Dominique had a classic case of 'trouble syndrome' which is a close cousin of the doom-mongering mind above, but focused and honed specifically to lure you into trouble spots, whispering in your ear of how wide the ditch is, how far the water and how deep the bunker. What most people, including Dominque, understandably try and do is ignore, suppress and stifle these unpleasant and unhelpful whisperings, but unfortunately this often has the opposite effect, fuelling and amplifying the thoughts further. It's like the old pink elephant trick: if you're told that you mustn't under any circumstances think about a pink elephant, then I guarantee your mind, previously entirely pink elephant free, will now crave so hard to think about one, that you'll have hundreds flying round your head before you know it – most annoying.

Dominique and I agreed to tackle the issue at source and visit his local course together. In the first few holes I was once again impressed with his skilled swing and confidence. He boomed his first drive over 300 yards down the fairway, made par, and on the second comfortably hit the green from 180 yards and made another easy par. At this point he looked more like a low handicap golfer than the official seventeen he was. However, the third hole started to bring home the problem, there was water all down the left-hand side, splash. The fifth hole the same, splash. The seventh hole needed a delicate lob shot over the bunker. Duff, the ball landed short in the bunker.

Dominique looked like a man defeated as we walked up the ninth. *I try my best to just ignore the water, but I'm so convinced it's going to go in, that it feels almost inevitable it will end up in there.* With this level of defeatist whispering dominating his thoughts, poor Dominique was stuck in a vicious circle of believing his ball would find the trouble, making it far more likely that it would end up there, which in turn strengthened the story further. And it's not just the mind that can play the troublemaker in this way, there will always be the odd person you play with who will deliberately bring the trouble to your mind. I have a friend who'd often point out the trouble, especially if he was losing – classic sledging! But there is a way to deal with it; it just requires a bit of reverse psychology. I remember one occasion when my friend politely pointed out the out-of-bounds down the right-hand side of the fairway as I was preparing to hit my driver. Embracing rather than shrinking from the thought, I took a good long look at it and commented back how vast the expanse was and how lucky we were to play in such beautiful surroundings. I then refocused, placing all my thoughts and gaze on a bush halfway down the middle of the fairway and preceded to hit a beautiful drive. *Wow, that was lucky*, I remarked, *it really does call your ball doesn't it? Anyway, your shot.* And yes, rather satisfyingly, on this occasion my friend did go on to hit it out of bounds, losing the hole and a few holes later the match. I think the key to countering the sledging was to confront it head on rather than retreating from it. It's a classic way to deal with a bully and works just as well on an internal bully as it does on an external one.

So, as we stood on the tenth fairway, looking down at a small lake in front of the green, it was time to confront Dominique's internal bully. I put my hand on his shoulder for a bit of moral support and suggested that he just have a good hard look at the water, at how wide it actually was, how deep, what club would be best to get over it. This was the first step to show Dominique's mind that it wasn't going to frighten us into ignoring the water and that we weren't going to rely on its overblown and pessimistic assessment of it anymore. The next step was to start to bring his trouble-making mind out into the open and actually acknowledge what it was saying. On this occasion, Dominique reported that it was basically a single phrase, *you're going in, you're going in, you're going in* on repeat inside his mind. We both laughed at the sheer negativity of it, which broke the tension, and seemed to reduce its power.

Next, I asked Dominque to re-focus his attention past the lake to the green behind it. To notice it in detail, from the cut of the grass, to the position of the hole, and to pick a very specific spot that he would like to aim for. That done, Dominique took up his position, and with one further look back at his spot, he swung, and effortlessly his ball rose up and well over the lake to land softly on the green. I've rarely seen a happier man than the one that turned towards me, raising his fist in defiance at his trouble-focused mind. We continued the round, and each time we encountered 'trouble' we went through the same routine of really seeing it with our own eyes and hearing the pessimistic predictions that his mind wanted him to believe, and then shifting his focus and hitting the shot. By the end of the round, he was animatedly talking to himself up the final fairway. *You see, that ditch wasn't so scary was it, you've just got to let go and let me get on with it. I know what I'm doing.* I was delighted. He'd begun to put that bully in its place – he now just needed to internalise the conversation or risk a different kind of ridicule from his friends!

Getting in the zone

It's not just doom-mongering or trouble-whispering thoughts that can get us into trouble on the course. Ironically positive thoughts can stymie us as well. I clearly remember the first time I experienced this. I'd been playing for a year or so and had quickly broken 100, 95, 90 and 85 but had yet to surpass 80 on the scorecard. Like so many of my early rounds, I was out on my own and even though I was playing for a score that day, I hadn't noticed how well I was doing until the seventeenth. I'd just hit a really nice drive finishing dead centre of the fairway and it was as I was waiting for the group in front to finish that I found myself working my score out and realising that I could actually break the magic 80 here. *If you just make a five here and a five at eighteen,* my mind whispered to me, *you'll shoot 79. Wow,* I began to think, *that will be amazing. I can't wait to tell my friends, I can start to think about shooting 75, I wonder how long it will take,* and so on. I was now so far away from being 'in the zone' or 'the moment', whatever you want to call it, that before I knew it I'd sleepwalked through the last few shots and finished seventeen with a 6 and eighteen with a 7, signing for 82. Yes, I may have equalled my best score, but I was bitterly disappointed and angry with my mind for distracting me.

This was a typical rookie error, I allowed myself to be carried off by my thoughts, transported to a glowing future rather than focusing on what I needed to do in the present. I've got a way of managing this particular one now: I've found that if I can catch myself before I'm too far into the daydream, then I can call myself back, thank my mind for the lovely vision, and persuade it that I'd actually be better off just focused on the next shot thank you very much. I do try and be fairly respectful to my mind on the course ... It's unruly, sometimes rude and very distracting, but it's not to blame. That's just what minds do.

Finding the flow

It doesn't happen very often, but there are magical times on the course when I manage to lose my mind (in a good way), to leave it behind or transcend it perhaps, and just be fully and totally absorbed in what I'm doing. The first time I remember having this sense of total absorption was during a club tournament as a young amateur. I was completely and utterly 'in' each shot, each hole, each moment, it was as if my vision grew sharper, my focus tighter and I just knew exactly what I needed to do. It was an almost out of body experience for me ... from which I awoke only after putting my ball into the hole on the eighteenth green and realising that I'd won the tournament.

I wish I could have bottled the 'flow' state I found that day. I'd certainly be a good deal richer than I am now. But sadly, I don't think you can chase after this kind of immersion, it's too mercurial or magical for that ... What I can say is that the times I've managed to find this flow state were ones when my mind was even and calm and quiet.

Sometimes that's been down to things outside of my control, like when the landscape I've played in is just so profoundly beautiful that my mind is transfixed and focused, or when I'm so happy and relaxed, absorbed in conversation with a good friend, that my mind takes its eye off the golf and lets me get on with it. But sometimes, like the day of the tournament, I've found this calmness of mind through the discipline and focus of having a very clear, set routine before each shot. My routine isn't particularly profound ... I simply take a couple of smooth, short practice swings, before stepping behind the ball to focus on the shot I want to hit. After a couple of deep breathes to release tension, I take my position. I take one last look at my target, do a weird little hip shuffle (don't ask me why) and the rest, as they say, is history.

There's something about the religious repetition of these simple motions that has become a calming ritual for me. It helps to slow everything from my heart rate to my swing right down, which in turn soothes and quietens my mind. From the little meditation that I've tried, I think the focus on breathing is designed to have a similar effect, to anchor the mind, and in so doing, release it from the endless barrage of thinking.

It's not a guarantee of course, but calm the mind and that wonderful state of zen, flow, or simply 'peace' can follow, elevating a round of golf from a nice pastime to something more profound, a chance to truly let go of day-to-day worries, to be unyoked from life and restored, for a few holes at least.

CHAPTER EIGHT

A Quick Tale from the Range

Practicing off the course

I read a book recently about practicing ... it said that anyone can become an expert at anything if they put in 10,000 hours of practice. I love this idea, that everything is open to everyone, and that all that stands between us and expertise is time and effort. And never has there been a truer example of this than with golf. I'm not suggesting you've got to put in 10,000 hours, but I've genuinely never met a client who didn't improve their game with practice. As Lee Trevino once said, *The more I practice the luckier I get.*

When our son turned three, it became abundantly clear from the carpet divots and broken ornaments that he had outgrown whacking plastic golf balls around the house. It was time for a trip to our local club to hit some real golf balls. So, we decided to visit Hazlemere, the club where I spent many happy years as an assistant pro, and where Luke Donald learnt his trade. It's a relaxed and friendly course, and I knew they wouldn't mind my son going out on the course, so we collected our golf bags and trotted happily off towards the pro shop. My son noticed the buggies, or little cars as he put it, parked outside the shop, and was immensely excited to discover that we were going to drive one round the golf course – in fact I think this was his favourite bit of the whole experience. We started off on the practice ground where he hit ball after ball like a machine gun, shelling bullets not particularly bothered where they went, just enjoying the act of hitting. And then we were off on the first, a look of delight on his face as we bumped down the hill in the buggy. We ended up playing about thirteen very short makeshift holes and drawing a number of dinosaurs in various bunkers. He was impeccably behaved, apart from a brief temper tantrum at my refusal to follow his request to drive the buggy into the pond by the third green. I couldn't have been more proud as we headed for the club house for a well-earned lunch.

After that first trip, we've regularly visited the course when it's quiet on a Wednesday afternoon, and we've also taken to visiting the local driving range. We have a nice routine of saying hello to the friendly pro before my son presses the button to release the balls into his bucket, which he very carefully carries to his bay, and hits them all as fast as possible before going back for more. After that we take our sandwiches and go and sit in the little café, where the pro very kindly lets him play with all the different coloured golf balls. It's a very relaxed, very happy time we spend together. I try my best not to go on too much about what to do, and just allow him to learn himself. I always want golf to be a choice for him, not a chore or something he's expected to do.

Anyway, it was on one of these visits to the range when we happened to be in a bay next to a young woman hitting some balls. In between telling my son that roaring like a T-rex isn't usually the thing to do at the range, and congratulating him on his shots, I noticed that the woman didn't seem to be having much fun. Now granted, this could have partly been due to us being noisy neighbours, but she didn't seem focused on us, more the other people around us. It certainly was busy – mostly men, mostly trying to hit their drivers as far as possible.

Now I'm used to this sort of environment, but I can still remember the apprehension the first time I set foot on a range and was confronted with approximately fifty people stood in tiny little booths whacking balls into the night sky. I remember how intimidating it felt to find my spot in amongst these seemingly seasoned golfers, and the humiliation I felt the first time I used the ball dispenser, and forgot to put my bucket underneath the shoot – having to rush around, apologising and picking up balls from beneath golfers feet! So I had some empathy for how our neighbour in the next bay might be feeling.

I try not to watch other people's golf when I'm 'off duty' but I couldn't help hearing the sharp knock as the woman's ball hit the side of our booth. Don't worry at all, I said as she offered her apologies. There were also a couple of mishits, and I could hear her sighing and looking around with what seemed extreme discomfort. Soon, the man on the other side had noticed too, and was quite obviously watching as she continued her practice, before beginning to offer something of a commentary, *Ooh, unlucky one, try again* that kind of thing, before moving on to offer suggestions on what she might try differently.

I don't know what the woman thought of this unsolicited commentary, but I felt livid. It seemed like such a patronising thing to do, assuming she needed or wanted his help and piling pressure on her to perform. No one else on the range was subject to this sort of attention, apart from my son, who attracted various onlookers commenting on his enthusiasm and enquiring about his age.

Now, I think it is one thing to offer commentary on a child's performance, quite another to do so on a fellow golfer, who just happens to be a young woman. I'm sure this man meant no harm and was probably trying to make her feel more at home, but I do think it's one of the problems, particularly for beginners and particularly for women, who want to practice on the range. You are very exposed, everyone can see and judge, which can make it a pretty difficult environment to learn. Unless of course you are three and totally oblivious.

The woman ran out of balls, and politely thanked the man for his help and left the range ... I wondered if she'd ever come back. We also finished up and went home. I felt torn, part of me wished that I had told her she'd done fine and to just ignore the rest of us and do her own thing ... but I guess that would have added to the problem of men feeling the need to comment on her experience.

Practicing anything is hard, particularly a game like golf where the movement needed is quite alien from our everyday actions and so can feel very awkward and inconsistent to begin with. It takes discipline and commitment to do something awkward again and again until you're good at it. But the things that you can do with practice! From being an ungainly mess on the slopes I can now ski a red run. In my adult life I've also mastered cooking, swimming, surfing – ok mastered may be pushing it, but there are all these things that I couldn't do, that I can now do and enjoy, all thanks to practice. And the wonderful thing I've found about practice is the more I do it, the easier it becomes, and the more motivated I become to keep going ... the joy of little moments of success. So, I guess I'm saying that practising is a really important thing to do, and worth taking some time to think about how to do it. So, for what it's worth, here are my thoughts.

Different kinds of practice

The word practice came from the Latin word 'to do', and that is essentially what I'm talking about here ... 'doing' lots of golf will make you better. But without meaning to overcomplicate, I think there are different kinds of doing. There's the thinking bit of doing, when you consider, discuss and take ownership of what it is you are trying to do in the first place – this bit is usually what you get when you go for a golf lesson, or certainly what you get if you come to see me.

Then there's the learning bit of doing, when you school the movements of golf, and finally the performing bit of doing when you're out on the course actually playing golf. All parts of the doing of golf are worth practicing, but if asked where to start I'd suggest with the thinking and the learning. If you can understand clearly what it is you are trying to do, then you'll get the most out of learning the movements of golf, and if you've learnt the movements of golf, you'll be well set to practice the performing of golf.

Practicing the movement of golf

Think of golf like a martial art ... You start off practicing a series of movements again and again, slowly building your muscle memory so that the motion feels natural and smooth. In so doing, you learn what each movement is for, and begin to understand how each can be used. Only then do you introduce a sparring partner, and put some of those movements into practice.

I think golf is best practiced in a similar way. You can begin to teach your body the series of connected movements needed to execute the swing – no ball, and not even a club, is needed to begin to school this motion, strengthening the muscles, increasing suppleness and finding a rhythm and consistency to the movements. Once this feels familiar, practicing with the ball becomes more important, as you put into practice the feelings and movements you've been schooling.

Now, I'm not Mr Miyagi, and I'm not suggesting as he did in the Karate Kid that you have to focus on the thinking and learning stages for months before performing the movements with a ball. On the contrary, hitting golf balls is essentially what is required to play the game, and obviously the more balls you hit successfully, the more confidence you gain for the course. But what I would say is that taking the time to get used to the feeling of the movement of the body when you swing is well worth it.

It only takes a few minutes each day to practice with the body, repeating the motion again and again until it starts to feel comfortable, repeatable and becomes natural. This is what I call 'grooving' your swing ... The repetition of the body's movement will carve out a pathway both in your brain but also in your muscle memory, creating a blueprint if you like, so that it becomes second nature. That way, when a ball is put in front of you, bringing with it all its temptations to hit, and the anxieties it can generate, you have something to fall back on, something reliable and solid and consistent. Your body knows what to do, even if the ball – rather like an opponent in a martial art – fuddles the mind and confuses the soul.

Allow time for incubation

They say time heals, but I think it also improves. Now, you could say that as my birthdays rack up, it is rather to my advantage to hold this view. But there is something in it ... in fact something almost magical about the way you can get better at something from one day to the next. One day my son couldn't ride a bike, the next he nearly did it, and the day after that he rode down the middle of the road cheering! I think what's happening here is that between each practice there's a rest period, in which the unconscious mind begins processing the experience, helping to reinforce and consolidate the feeling being practiced. As a man of science once said to me, *A good night's sleep is an efficient way to help bring clarity to confusion.*

So, allowing time for your practice at home to incubate is really important, and means that you can be improving your golf even in your sleep. It also means that when you do get to affirm the feeling on the range or perform golf out on the course, you can allow yourself to forget the thinking or learning practice that you've been doing. You can just concentrate on enjoying the game, trusting that the work you've put in will naturally shape the way you play.

Using the range

By far the best place to practice the 'performing' of golf is on the course, as you get to practice hitting balls from all sorts of different positions and lies. The driving range is absolutely not a substitute for the course, but it does have its place. I see the range as a chance to affirm the feelings you've been practicing at home. This is a very different aim from how most people use the range ... Your average golfer waits until they're at the range to try and remember, process and then deliver the movements they've been learning, which is quite frankly a tall order. And to make it even harder for themselves, they tend to practice 'performing' golf by which I mean that their focus is on where the ball goes rather than on what their body is doing or the feeling of the swing.

There is nothing wrong with this extremal rather than internal focus if you're not in the early stages of learning a feeling. In fact, the range can be a fun place if all you're thinking about is trying to hit various shots or hit the targets placed out on the range. But it's too soon to focus on where the ball is going if you're trying to process the new feelings and movements of the swing. It will only be disappointing and probably frustrating, so instead, keep with the feeling and the result will come.

Holding this internal focus in mind when you visit a range can be a bit of challenge, as there is inevitably some pressure to 'conform' to the need to perform ... it can be quite a competitive place. With this in mind, I always advise my clients to visit the range when it's likely to be quiet, and to pick a bay at the very end so you're not constantly looking at what others are doing, and equally, others aren't as likely to get involved with what you're doing. If this sounds essentially antisocial, then I make no apologies for it!

The next thing I'd advise is to practice with just one club – the club you feel most comfortable and familiar with. Trust me, it's a lot easier to affirm and grow confidence with a new feeling using one club rather than a host of different ones.

And remember to really try not to focus on where the balls end up. I know it's very tempting, but instead, notice the feeling you create when you swing the club, notice your position, be mindful of each shot. This will help stop you falling into a bad range habit of hitting multiple balls back to back without ever actually reflecting on what you're doing.

I realise that this is beginning to sound a bit like a nagging parent telling you all the things you should or shouldn't do ... but bear with me, even nagging parents have sometimes got a point! So, ploughing on, try not to be too hard on yourself, you'll never be able to exactly replicate the feeling of movement you had at home, because you'll naturally be more ball focused, but at least you have a blueprint to work towards. And finally(!) set yourself a ball limit, and even if it's not going well, rather like poker, walk away when you're out of money/balls.

CHAPTER NINE

In Your Life Have You Seen Anything Like That!

The mercurial magic of the short game

If the swing to golf is like breathing to living, then the short game is like our capacity to think and feel. It's the part of the game where we most use our uniquely human capacities to strategize, to plan, to imagine, to be creative, audacious and bold. The short game has given us some of the most magical shots in the long history of the game of golf. Indeed, this is the part of the game that infuses the sport with a mercurial fascination – it is the part most likely to win your heart but also to break it. It is my favourite part of the game, and I feel very protective of it ... Too often it is neglected or overlooked, caught between the twin powers of the drive and the putt. So here I set the balance right, and present to you my ode to the short game.

A few years ago now, a young man started visiting *Urban Golf*, hitting balls for half an hour or so, grabbing some lunch and then heading out again. I noticed him one day when I had a gap in my lessons and happened to walk past his booth. I was struck by his rather stylish and assured swing, approaching each shot in a calm and content manner, he didn't appear to be thinking or analysing, but instead just allowed his body and swing to move with a natural flow. There was such a confidence to the movement that there was just no doubt that he was going to hit a beautiful shot – it was a pleasure to watch.

I was intrigued, who was this young man who seemed to have such poise and control. Was he a professional? Where did he play? I found myself full of curiosity and took the rather forward step of introducing myself and telling him how much I liked his style. He seemed both surprised and pleased by my praise, told me his name was Rishi, and invited me to hit some balls with him over the lunch hour.

As I learnt more about him, my admiration for him grew. He'd only been playing for nine months and had not yet set foot on a course, instead practicing at the range and *Urban Golf*. More surprising still was the fact that he was entirely self-taught, having learnt from watching golf on the TV. An architect by trade, he told me he'd always been quite sporty, but with golf had very quickly felt like it was a good fit for him and had taken to it like the proverbial duck to water.

Over the months, Rishi and I continued to meet for the odd lunchtime chat, and on occasion played a few holes, utilising Urban's collection of digitised courses to play St Andrews, Pebble Beach, all the greats. And it was when we started to play rather than just hit some balls that the gaps in my friend's game became all too apparent. He'd start off great from the tee, often ending up ahead of me down the fairway, but that's when it changed dramatically.

These shorter shots within about 50 yards of the hole need care, thought, concentration, but Rishi seemed to choose his short club almost at random, and very quickly take his shot, seemingly with little care where it would end up. Honestly, it was like watching a completely different golfer, so wide was the gulf between his short and long game. And the effect on his score was plain for all to see. With a swing like his, he was easily headed for a single figure handicap, but once you added up all the shorter shots including the mishits, shots dribbling along the ground, or soaring way over the green, he was doubling or tripling his score, taking him out of the handicap range all together.

And this isn't an issue unique to Rishi; there's a lot of

golfers out there who develop their fuller swing and get to a point where this feels really comfortable and consistent but neglect the shorter shots that actually get the ball on the green and close to the hole. I think the mistake is in thinking that these are 'add ons' or nice extras rather than crucial tools that help bring the whole game together

This was powerfully brought home to me early in my career when I took a playing lesson with a prestigious golf pro to learn how I could take my golf to the next level and turn pro. I remember being incredibly nervous, so keen was I to impress him with my swing that I could hardly move the club off the first, but I managed to pull it together and hit some pretty nice shots in the end – he still beat me, but not by much.

Afterwards he turned to me and told me that I'd done well, but that if I wanted to take my game to the next level, I'd need to develop my short game rather than keep focusing just on my full swing. He told me that the only secret to golf is to understand that the game is won or lost not from the tee, but from within 50 yards of the hole.

I vividly remember him telling me that he'd got a whole arsenal of short shots that he'd developed over the years to get him out of tight spots, over water, out of bunkers, from behind trees, and that's why he'd always beat me. *If you want to get better*, he told me, *work on your short game and increase the number of shots you're able to play with your wedge, that's how your handicap will drop away and you can start to cut your score.*

And you know what, I took his advice. I stopped spending hours on the range hitting five irons and I put that energy into developing my short game. In fact, I ended up spending most of my practice time honing and inventing a vast array of shorter shots in and around the green. I was like a kid in a toy shop. This new kind of creative and chaotic practice was fun, and it made me love the game even more. A few years later I got to play regular golf with this pro and not only did I get the chance to show off my skills to him but on occasion I even beat him!

Now, Rishi wasn't a client of mine. He'd become a friend and I was rather reluctant to get into coaching him, but after one particularly disastrous par three I remember asking him what exactly was going on with his short game. *I just can't be bothered with it*, he said, *I just find these short shots so dull and I can't seem to find any feel to them.* Well, I can tell you I was more outraged and horrified than if he'd told me there was no such thing as climate change.

How could this beautiful swinger of the club think so little of the best part of the golf game. I just couldn't understand it. And then it struck me, of course, this was a golfer who had literally never been out on the course.

The short game on the range, even with the brilliant high-tech imagery of golf courses available at *Urban Golf*, just can't do justice to the short game. It can't capture the feeling of being 10 yards off the green, the ball nestled deep down in the grass with a bunker lying between you and the hole, and deciding to hit an audacious high shot up over the bunker so it drops dead still next to the flag. Or the brilliant combination of imagination and instinct as you figure out the exact point on the green on which to chip the ball to capture the break and have the ball trickle down beside the hole. Yes, it may be more subtle than the raw dynamism of the drive, but there is treasure here – I just had to help Rishi find it.

Ok, I said, getting my phone out, *watch this ...* I played him the legendary clip from the 2005 final round of the Masters. Tiger Woods is leading the Masters by one shot as he tees off on the par-three sixteenth. His ball lands long and left at the bottom of the enormous green, just at the boundary with the second cut of rough. The pin is positioned precariously above him to the back left of the sloping green, the grass cut so short that it's as slippery as black ice. The commentator sounds anxious, *This is one of the toughest pitches on the entire place here*.

With the crowd deadly silent, Tiger stands over the ball, a look of intense concentration and determination on his face, considering the lie, the feel, the pitch. Of all the millions of shots he'd played before, there could have been none exactly like this ... like a chess player, he was having to compute all of what he had learnt before, and then go beyond replication, to visualise and then create something new and original for this exact moment, this exact time.

And he did. He struck the ball, sending it low, skipping up the slope far above and to the left of the hole, bouncing on a ridge in the green and then turning and beginning a slow descent down towards the hole. *Oh my goodness*, the commentator cries above the excitement of the crowd as the ball draws closer, and stops, teetering on the edge before it falls, smooth as butter into the hole. The crowd explode with cheers, Tiger leans back, fists clenched, the commentator sums in up, *Oh wow! In your life have you seen anything like that?* It was a shot of wonder, of majesty, of hope – it was one of the most incredible moments the game has seen before or since. I put down my phone, grinning and looked at Rishi. *The short game is not boring*, I said. He grinned back. *Ok, I take your point, you've got to show me how to do that!*

Two weeks later, Rishi caught the train out of London, I picked him up and drove him out to my favourite inland course, Ley Hill. It's a tight, wooded nine-hole course, with beautiful undulating fairways, and a relaxed, open policy. After playing the first three holes Rishi and I set up camp on the fourth hole, a beautiful par-three dropping steeply down a gulley, with two bunkers and a wall of trees shielding the sloping green on three sides. It's a perfect place to practice all sorts of short-game shots.

As we walked down, I gave him just two pieces of advice, which was to keep his grip soft and use his arms rather than his body to create the motion of the swing. Unlike the longer shots, I said, where you use your body to facilitate the swing, for the short game, the body can stay nice and quiet and act as an anchor for the arms to play the different shots. That is literally all I told him, other than to have fun, experiment and just practice getting the ball as close to the hole any way that he could.

Well, we practiced them all. From high sweeping lobs, to little chips that spun and checked as they hit the green, to precision chips that just got the ball far enough to use the slope to roll down to the hole. We weren't practicing 'standard' shots like you do on the range but were figuring out the shots as we went, using ball after ball to understand what happens when you hit it with the toe end of the club, with the face open and closed, with our feet together or apart, with the ball at the front and back of our stance. It was a lot of fun, in a geeky golfer kind of a way. We must have hit hundreds of balls, with the shot of the day going to Rishi after he holed an audacious lob from the bottom of a bank over a bush!

By the end of it, Rishi had really understood that the short game is not about learning particular golf shots that you then reproduce on the course. It's about understanding what you need to do in each particular position to get your ball either in or as close as you can to the hole. This means learning to visualise the shot, understanding how the ball is likely to travel, where it's likely to land and what it will do when it hits the green. And the only way to get a feel for what the ball will do is to practise loads of different shots, from loads of different lies, or in other words, to just be creative and mess around and find your own short game – there really is no better way to learn.

As we sat in the club house later, sipping a cold beer, I told Rishi a story about one of my most memorable chips. It was a fair few years ago, when I was a lot cockier and possibly stupider ... a couple of other pros and I were playing at the legendary Turnberry Golf Club in Scotland. We'd had a wonderful game and were messing around in the lodge before dinner. We'd arranged a small wager: who was brave enough to pitch a ball over the bed and out through one of the bay windows? I was pretty confident with my short game at that time and took on the bet. Choosing my trusty Hogan 56 degree wedge and channelling my concentration on a flag I could see in the distance through the window, I made the shot, which soared up beautifully over the bed, past the tv and the sofa, and out through the open window, plopping harmlessly on the grass in front. Call it luck or judgment, I don't know, but thankfully no windows were broken that day and I made a bit of money too.

Incidentally, this took place before Turnberry was acquired by a certain US 'celebrity' ... I wonder to myself whether I'd be quite so careful if I took that wager again today.

CHAPTER TEN

The Golden Rule

The principles behind the game

'Ethics is what we do when no one else is looking.'

Frasier Crane, *Frasier*, 'To tell the Truth'

I've never been one for rules ... I think I equate rules with an infringement of my freedom, and constantly strive to live a life that isn't weighted down by too many 'shoulds' or 'musts' or, even worse, 'must nots'.

Given golf's reputation as stuffy, fussy and rule laden, you may well think that I have chosen my career very poorly if I want to live as a free spirit. And, you've got a point ... there are a good few rules governing the playing of the game, and a fair few more about what to wear, how to behave, even which part of the club house you're allowed in with golf shoes on. Most of the 'off-course' rules I think are a bit ridiculous, and some of them have been used to justify blatant discrimination and exclusion – there are still clubs in the UK where women are not omitted to all the club house rooms, and of course it was only in 1990 that Augusta admitted its first African American member, and 2012 its first female member.

Appalling I know, but perhaps not surprising when you remember that golf is a very old sport. This is no bad thing; in fact in brings rich depth to the game, but also means that the rules and regulations were developed in a past era which was intrinsically racist and sexist. The upshot is that the underlying structures, like so many of our institutions, are engrained in outdated and discriminatory practices. But thank goodness that's not the end of the story. Golf is modernising and innovating and becoming more open and inclusive, and with that, some of the outdated rules are being overturned, some of the old practices done away with.

And what's left, the core of the rules for playing the game I have no problem with. I want to be a free spirit, not an anarchist, and so I've found that as long as I can avoid clubs, competitions and golfers who think 'exclusive' means 'exclusion', 'tradition' means 'stuck in the past', and 'standards' means 'arbitrary rules and pettiness', the rules of golf and I have rubbed along pretty well.

Look after the course

When I was a junior, I often had the pleasure to play with a lovely older member called Arnold. He was a very kind man and always took the time to say hello to us younger members and to make us feel included and welcome at the club. He took me under his wing and taught me all sorts, probably the most powerful of which was that my putter had an off switch. He was a quiet, slow talking, slow walking kind of a man. He'd do things at his pace and in his own way. I remember one of the things I found a bit irritating playing with him to start with was the time and attention he'd give to little things like replacing a divot or tee mark. He'd spend ages carefully positioning the divot back in its hole, delicately pressing it down on all four sides, and then tapping his putter over the entire surface, before he was satisfied and proceeded down the fairway. He took the same care and pleasure when he'd rake a bunker, removing both his own foot marks, and those of the many golfers preceding him who hadn't felt the need to make such an effort. He also, as a matter of course, carried an empty plastic bag around with him to pick up any discarded crisp packets or water bottles he found along the way. He didn't make a big deal out of it, just methodically and carefully cared for and preserved the course. I didn't think much of it beyond that he was slow and I wanted to get on with the playing. But I think those early rounds seeped into my unconscious in a way that's stayed with me my whole life. I'm now the one carefully sprinkling the mixture of sand and grass seed over the tee box, working it in to the diverts of not just my own, but an assortment of missed holes and dents along the way. I'm the one who can spend a happy few minutes going over the green with the toe of my putter, smoothing down and stabilising pitch marks – I think that old member would be proud of me.

It's a habit that I'd formed early on and I distinctly remember being teased by the other juniors as a goody goody following the rules as I brought up the rear down the fairway to ensure all divots were back in their grassy beds. I was pretty horrified by the accusation. The last thing I wanted to do was follow rules, but I did care, I cared deeply about looking after the course. And that's the way that I think I've learnt to rub along so well with the rules of golf ... I don't follow any rule for the sake of it, I follow rules that have an underlying foundation that makes sense to me.

The rules that really matter

In the rather dense document produced by the Royal & Ancient on the rules of golf, there's a short introductory bit which includes three 'standards of players conduct'.

These are to act with integrity, to show consideration to others and look after the course. Personally I think that if golfers focused more on these three principles, rather than getting lost in the detail of the rules, then the game would be better for it. As Aristotle said, if we slavishly follow rules with no real understanding, then we're likely to lose our way in a tricky situation where the rule no longer apply, but if we try to really know and understand what is the right thing to do, then we can live a truly virtuous life. And if that's good enough for life, then it's good enough for golf.

Consideration for others

The hypocrisy of rules was perfectly and sadly illustrated to me when my friend and work colleague Kate and I decided to meet up on a Saturday to play golf, along with our girlfriends. Now Kate is an absolutely fabulous golfer, with an effortless easy swing which could easily have held its own on the professional women's circuit if she had wanted it to. Her girlfriend Emma had just taken up the game, but being naturally coordinated was going great guns and was already hitting the ball nicely. Helen was Helen, with her ability to hit it beautifully just as likely as she was to hit it out of bounds. We made up a happy four-ball, heading out in the later afternoon so we could take our time round the sunny, open course. It was on the fourth hole when we first saw the buggy with a rather austere looking man and his young son heading fast down the third. I think we were all in the rough at this point, and having a laugh finding our balls. We smiled and nodded at our fellow golfers. The acknowledgement wasn't retuned, but hey, maybe they hadn't seen us. We were on the seventh hole, going up adjacent to the sixth going down when Kate hit a lovely loping tee shot, that rather unfortunately ended up in some nasty rough down the edge of the hole. Kate, Emma and Helen went over to search for it, whilst I headed to the other side of the fairway for my ball. I turned as I heard raised voices. The same man and his son that we'd passed on the fourth were now heading towards Kate fast in the buggy, shouting at her to get off the course. I didn't catch it all, but it was along the lines of, *If you can't play the game, you shouldn't be here, ruining the game for everyone else.* I headed over quickly to find the man out of the buggy and remonstrating with Kate and the others that this was a member's club and the rules were there to be followed and this kind of thing wouldn't be tolerated. I gather that 'this kind of thing' referred to Kate looking for her ball. I asked the man what the problem was, and that I was a golf pro accompanying my friends round the course. He suggested I find another place to teach, and screeched off in his buggy, his young son looking sad and rather lost in the passenger seat.

We were all completely deflated and quite shaken up by the ferocity of this man's attack. What had we done wrong? What rule were we supposed to have broken? The fact is that Emma and Helen had been doing brilliantly, we hadn't held anybody up and we didn't take overly long to look for Kate's ball, so there really was nothing that the man could have objected to. I think the fact that three of us were female and that we'd twice been seen looking for balls in the rough, and had the audacity to be having fun, made this member jump to some kind of conclusion about our right to share the course with him, and he 'threw' the rules at us in an attempt to justify an intolerable position of discrimination. The ironic thing is that the only person who broke any rules that day was him … He broke the fundamental principle enshrined by the R&A to show consideration to others, and he should be entirely ashamed of himself.

But consideration goes further than live and let live, which is more than this man would suffer, and means having a real sense of respect and acceptance for everybody on the golf course, whether they be men or women, professionals or beginners. That doesn't mean doing very much in practice beyond the basics like ensuring you shout *FOUR* if your ball goes astray so that no one gets conked on the head. It might also mean saying hello to other golfers round the course and being aware of how your game is affecting others … So if you're a four-ball, consider letting the two ball behind you through rather than making them wait to commence each hole, if the course is busy and there are groups on each hole, consider dropping another rather than holding everyone up whilst you look for your ball in the heavy rough, or picking up your ball once there's a winner on the green. It might mean stopping to wait whilst others tee off, or lowering your voice and slowing your step when going past a group putting out. Most golfers would agree with these basic ideas, but the key is to maintain this same level of respect and thoughtfulness for everyone on the course ... So to let the two ball through even if they are older women who you assume you can play better than, waiting for a group to tee off even if they are beginners and the shots only trickle along the ground, lowering your voice when a group are putting, even if they are juniors, and saying hello even if the golfers aren't members. It's not rocket science, but it's amazing how many golfers fully versed in the rules of the game could do with a refresh.

Integrity

On the most basic interpretation, the R&A's principle 'to act with integrity' is about not cheating. I'm all for this. If you're going to score then obviously do it honestly, with yourself and others. And like I say to my son, *It's no fun playing the game if you're not going to follow the rules*, after his counter has miraculously climbed the snake whilst he insists mine falls down the ladder on his way to another dubious victory.

On the other hand, I think you can play with your integrity entirely intact and still pick up your ball from behind a tree and drop it somewhere more playable, take celebrity drops, replay shots, really whatever you like, as long as you're doing it out in the open and you're not playing in a competitive match. There are a fair few golfers out there who I think fundamentally misinterpret this and think that the only way to play is by competition rules. But there's nothing in the rules that says that every golf game should be a competition, so the logic is faulty, and as they say, if you live by the rules, then you've got to die with them too.

But I think the idea of playing with integrity is more than not cheating – you can refrain from cheating but still not play 'in the spirit' of the game. And that's where the idea of 'sportsmanship' comes in ... I see this as the practical arm of integrity, the root of which is summed up in the old saying, *It's not whether you win or lose, it's how you play the game.* So an example of sportsmanship is when a batsman walks off the field because they know the ball touched their bat even when the umpire missed it, or when a sprinter accidentally trips up a fellow runner and stops to help them up, it's about shaking hands with your opponent when you beat them, as well as when you are beaten. In golf, there's no better example of sportsmanship than that shown by Jack Nicholas on the last day of the 1969

Ryder Cup. The first two days had been somewhat contentious and ill tempered, marred by unsportsmanlike behaviour on both sides. And so tension was high on the final day as Jack Nicolas walked down the eighteenth, playing in the final pair with England's Tony Jacklin. The overall score was tied 15½ to the States, 15½ to Europe, and the pair were level coming down the eighteenth. Both ended up with short but miss-able second putts for par to halve the match and tie the tournament. Nicholas went first, and it went in. He then instantly picked up Jacklin's ball marker and said to him, *I don't think you would have missed it, but I wasn't going to give you the chance, either.* That act, to concede the putt, at the highest level of competition, was remarkable. It began a friendship that lasted a lifetime and helped set the bar for the tone and spirit of all Ryder cups which followed – I'll have to show the clip to my son sometime.

And it's not just on a grand scale that sportsmanship is relevant, in fact it happens every day on every course, up and down the country. Small acts of integrity like giving an early concession to a companion who's having a dreadful round, searching for the ball of your opponent at a critical point in a match or insisting on playing without scoring with a friend whose game has gone astray.

So I guess my message is to bend, duck and shimmy through all the rules you like, but never forget those values that make golf a game we can all be proud of. It's not difficult. In fact, you can sum it up by the so-called golden rule taught in primary schools around the country: treat others (and the course) how you'd like to be treated yourself. As I check the BBC website for the latest news, I wonder how such a simple and universal truth can be so difficult for us all to follow.

CHAPTER ELEVEN

No One Will Ever Forget That Twelve!

Measuring what matters

Judge Smails: Ty, what did you shoot today?
Ty Webb: Oh, Judge, I don't keep score.
Judge Smails: Then how do you measure yourself with other golfers?
Ty Webb: By height.

Caddy Shack, 1980

'As Bond handed his club to Hawker and strolled off in the wake of the more impatient Goldfinger, he smelled the sweet smell of the beginning of a knock-down-and-drag-out game of golf on a beautiful day in May with the larks singing over the greatest seaside course in the world.'

Goldfinger, by Ian Fleming

Over an anniversary dinner this summer, my wife and I were remembering our honeymoon. We both agreed it had been just the most amazing time, travelling round northern France in an open-top car, some nights staying in the height of luxury and eating gourmet food, others pulling into a camp site and cooking our meals over an open fire, with a fair bit of golf thrown in for good measure.

The funny thing was that our memories of the bits that made it amazing were quite different – my wife talked of the wonderful evening we sat in front of the sunset at a certain campsite, which frankly I couldn't quite bring to mind, whilst I fondly remembered a romantic windy walk up to a lighthouse which she recalls as being cold and wet. Luckily we hit upon the shared amazing memory of eating a rotisserie chicken on the beach, which revived the atmosphere a bit and we moved on.

But what strikes me about this slightly treacherous conversational terrain is how we could share exactly the same experience, both agree we had a wonderful time, but find that what mattered to us both was quite different. And so it is with golf – we're all nominally playing the same game, but why we're playing, what we're getting out of it and what we love (and hate) about it can be quite different.

There's a classic golf movie called *Tin Cup* in which Kevin Costner plays an irascible golf pro, eking out an existence on an out-of-town driving range. As we get to know him through the eyes of Rene Russo, playing his soon to be psychologist girlfriend, we see the insecurities, fears and swaggering bravado that we assume has kept him from professional success. But we also see something more fundamental – we see that what's important to him in the game of golf is beating the course, making the impossible shot, defying possibility. That's what motivates and drives him, not the winning or making money, but being audacious.

This plays out as the movie concludes and Kevin (or should I say Tin Cup) has rather surprisingly qualified for the US Open. He finds himself in joint lead on the final day as he drives down the final hole in a dog fight with his nemesis, a much more successful professional rival. Tin Cup then has a choice between an easy lay up which will very likely leave him a par and secure him the win, or an almost impossible 230 yard shot over the lake to finish the hole with an eagle.

Although he has already failed to make this same shot in the previous three rounds, he still decides to go for it. His first ball hits the green and then agonisingly, rolls back into the water... he goes for it again, and again and again ... he has one ball left in his bag, if this goes in the water he can't even turn in his card, let alone qualify for next year's open. He insists on going for it again, his caddy beyond furious, his psychologist girlfriend laughing rather manically in the crowd as she knows this is his true self manifest. He hits the last ball, it reaches the green, and rolls into the hole. He makes a 12 and loses the tournament, but as his girlfriend says, *No one will ever forget that twelve.*

Whether you applaud him or think he's out of his mind, I reckon the point of the movie is about staying true to yourself, and not compromising what matters to us in favour of what society judges is important. For Tin Cup, being the best golfer meant playing that shot, defining the moment, and that is what he did.

I think there's something in this – in our target-driven society it's difficult not to be 'taken in' by the illusion that success and enjoyment are defined by how others view us and assess us rather than by what matters to us. If we listen, society will judge how 'good' we are in every area of our life from our finances, employment and appearance to our competence as parents and even as lovers. But surely what matters more is what we think and feel about our own lives?

I've always thought of the golf club as a microcosm of society (albeit a more privileged and white-centric version – something else that needs to change) and as in life, there will always be someone to judge your game, to tell you what you're doing is wrong, to pronounce whether golf is for you or not. And so it feels like a good place to start to push back, to assert our own right to decide what matters to us. So before we jump to check our score card or consider whether we have won or lost, when asked the question *how did you play* perhaps we should first consider what it is that makes us tick ... what makes us play golf ... and then answer the question *how did you play* on our own terms and those alone.

What matters?

The people that I know who enjoy their golf the most are those that have figured out what it is they enjoy about the game and play purely for that reason. Take one of my closest friends, Swiss – he plays golf to be with his friends, and doesn't let anything get in the way of that aim. It's an almost purely social event for him and has been since he took it up when we all went golf crazy in our late teens.

Don't get me wrong, this doesn't mean he's no good at it. In fact, he's got rather a beautiful swing that on a good day can make the ball fly miles, and he very much enjoys *making the ball sing*, as he would say. But even when he was a member of a club, he never played competitions, didn't worry about handicaps and didn't care that much about his score or even the course he was playing. He bent the rules to suit his game, dropping extra balls and kicking balls out from behind trees. And he did this so that he could get on with what was actually important to him, and that was laughing and chatting to his good friends on the way round.

Swiss is always a wonderful conversationalist, and charms everyone he meets whether he's at work, down the pub or on my sofa, but there's something about the rhythm of conversation on a golf course that makes it our favourite place to chat. We can have a quick catch up down the fairway, followed by snippets on the green between shots and then a more leisurely talk between holes, with Swiss telling stories, making me laugh, engaging in a bit of light sledging, mixed in with the odd moment of real sharing that somehow we never quite get around to without the golf course as our chaperone. For Swiss, I think golf is cathartic. He's never had a particularly straightforward life, and so golf gives him the chance for a good two hours of talk, digesting and making sense of his life with people who love him.

Writing this makes me realise how many months it is since we played together, the weight of his responsibilities makes golf seem a 'luxury' rather than a priority in his life right now. But remembering what it all meant to us both makes me think I've got to call him up and get him back out there. Those weren't idle times, just because he wasn't 'improving' or winning didn't mean it didn't count. On the contrary, I think our chats and time together on the course were far more important than the golf.

My wife gets rather a bad press in this book. I've detailed both her stubbornness and her over-ambition in some detail, and to add to her list of sins I'm now going to talk about her old-fashioned primness. That's right, my wife brings to golf the rigid attention to playing 'correctly' of a Victorian English school mistress.

When we first met, she'd have none of these new-fangled inventions like rescue clubs. If she was going to play the game, she'd get a good honest collection of irons and do it properly, no short cuts thank you very much. I've had a few clients express views in this direction, but Helen took it to an extreme, considering the use of this club to be cheating. Her funny ideas about what mattered went as far as refusing to use a putter off the green, her stubborn commitment to correctness meaning that to this day she will always select her wedge, regardless of whether it is a hair-brained decision.

I've done my best to erode these misguided commitments, and she has now deigned to carry a (barely used) rescue club in her bag, but I've never made headway with the wedge/putter debate, and getting her to consider using a celebrity drop was an uphill struggle. The fact is that Helen likes playing golf in this way; it matters to her that she keeps a proper score card even if it upsets her at the end. She likes the fact that she can rely on her irons, and she loves a high wedge onto the green, even when it runs off the other side ... Doing things properly is important to her, and she loves to embrace the traditions of the game, even wearing brown and white spats to play in, and I think if I hadn't made it abundantly clear it was a make or break issue, would have invested in a pair of plus 4s! And if that's what matters to her, then so be it, each to their own ... And somehow, her own and my own fit in a funny sort of way.

If Judge Smail asked me, as he did Ty Webb, how I measured myself against other golfers, my reply would have changed significantly over the years. But one thing is constant: at five foot nine, height would never be my measure of choice.

In the early days, the thing that mattered above all else to me was to reduce my handicap. In fact I lived and breathed it – I was obsessed with shaving shots off my score. And I think it was very good for me. As an early teen I'd never really committed to anything ... I wasn't particularly engaged or interested at school, and distinctly remember rocking up the first day of my GCSEs oblivious to the fact that I was about to sit an exam. I liked photography, football and tennis, but not in a fanatical way ... it wasn't till I found golf that passion stirred in me. This was something I understood, and that I was good at and that I desperately wanted to be better at. It gave me focus, purpose and ambition ...

I was something of a wandering soul before golf claimed me.

The first few years working at my handicap were certainly the easiest and probably some of the most enjoyable as I managed to reduce it down pretty quickly to 5. I won quite a few club competitions on the way down, many with what I look back on now as embarrassingly low net scores. The most wonderful/ embarrassing moment at the time was collecting a trophy for one club competition with a net 58. A feat I couldn't repeat now even using a bag full of celebrity drops. I wonder now how the members must have mumbled.

Things got tougher though when I reached a 5, as the handicap system dictates that the route to the promised land of 'scratch' be slower and harder. But all the same I still measured myself by my handicap and learnt to enjoy what was a different kind of challenge, a battle to play to my handicap even when the going was tough, and it was this grit and determination that allowed me to drop my handicap a few more shots.

After that my whole focus turned to becoming a professional. The image I had for my life was drawn almost directly from the relaxed life of the pro in *Caddy Shack:* teaching the odd lesson, playing occasional competitions, messing around in the pro shop and spending the rest of the time just playing golf. It wasn't the most ambitious vision, I must admit. I never really aspired to greatness, playing alongside my heroes on the international circuit. I guess it was just never my central mission – I love to play, I only like to win, and that was never going to be enough. But this lack of story for myself beyond turning pro meant that I think I lost sight of what mattered to me in playing golf for a few years and lost the joy a little bit. As it dawned on me how limited and restricted the teaching of golf was, I found my new passion and focus: to innovate and radically improve the teaching of the game. Since then I guess what's mattered to me is less about my own performance than that of my clients. If I can help them achieve their own version of success, then I'm very happy.

A wonderful side effect for me of this shift in focus is that it's freed me up to play golf with a new joy. What matters now to me is purely the beauty of the game. I play for the freedom I feel when I hit a weightless and effortless three iron that projects the ball beautifully up and on to the middle of the fairway. I play for the satisfaction of hitting as many shots as it takes to find the feeling that I want, rather than worry about where it goes. I have the confidence to play a whole round only with irons because I feel like it, and the audacity to use a celebrity drop if I don't feel like hoiking it out of the rough. There is no need to compete, to score, to measure myself against other golfers. I just play for the love of playing.

Measure what matters

I think there are really only two things you need to know to enjoy golf. The first is to understand what really matters to you about the game and the second and last step is to then make sure you only judge your game by that standard. Now, this might sound quite straightforward and obvious, but I can't tell you how many clients I've known who play golf primarily to be with friends or for a bit of exercise, but still feel compelled to measure themselves by their score card, and judge their day to be a success or failure on that basis rather than on whether they enjoyed their time.

So, I call on you all to throw off the shackles of societal expectation. Repel the judgement of well-meaning observers. This is your chance, your moment in history, to stand up and say, I will play golf on my own terms!

If, like James Bond, what matters to you is all about the competition, judge yourself by whether you win or lose the match, not by your net score. If you love the personal challenge of playing to your handicap, don't worry if half your shots go along the ground. If you got it down there and in the hole, it still counts. If, like me, it's all about the beauty of the game, then focus on how the shot feels rather than where it goes. If you just love whacking it miles, than whack it miles, and if it all goes pear shaped closer to the green, then don't stress, and if it's more about being outside for a bit of exercise, then be at peace with your standard of golf and check your pedometer steps instead.

Putting it into practice

For the majority of the things that matter to people about playing golf, scoring in any way is irrelevant. So, that means that for the majority of golfers I'd really really encourage you to not do it. Do not pick up a score card and do not score, even mentally, because keeping any sort of a tally will filter through and infiltrate your senses, impacting your enjoyment. You may have to be quite strict at reminding yourself why you're playing and what actually matters to you, be that friends, exercise or beauty.

For the remainder of you, it seems that part of what matters to you is how 'well' you play, either judged against your own performance or that of a competitor. And the wonderful thing about golf is that it's actually brilliantly set up to allow golfers to define what playing 'well' means along a continuum. In other words, 'well' in golf doesn't mean having to compare your each and every shot to that of Tiger Woods, thank goodness.

First of all, there's the handicap system, which allows golfers of very different abilities to play together, something which, if you think about it, is unheard of in practically all other sports. But that's not all, there are also different scoring systems that you can use to suit what matters to you. So, if you're one of the relatively small percentage of golfers who really wants to work on reducing their handicap, then play stroke play. You simply count each shot you take to get the ball in the hole. This is the harshest scoring method, and I really wouldn't recommend it unless you're a regular and dedicated handicap golfer.

If on the other hand you love a good person-on-person competition, then using the match play scoring system might work for you. Here, each hole is either won or lost depending upon who got it in the hole in net fewer shots, that is, after their handicap has been taken into account. It's a good method for equally competitive and combative golfers! And the great thing about this method is that once a hole has been won, the other can just pick up their ball, no need to keep going to the bitter end.

Probably my favourite method of scoring (if I score at all, which isn't often nowadays) is called Stableford. This is a great way to both keep track of how you're playing personally and still compete as in match play. But rather than the cut and dry, win or lose system for each hole, here there's a point system: 2 points for a par, 3 for a birdie, 1 for a bogie and 0 for any score above. The nice thing about this system is that you can still score if you are 1 or even 2 shots over your handicap, which is ideal for the occasional or inconsistent golfer, golfers without a handicap or the nervous competitor. It means that you can still get a respectable score on your card when in match play it might read *lost, lost, lost,* and

Stableford has the decency of recording just an innocent 0 for what in stroke play might read a 9. You see the advantage!

And of course, these are not the only ways you can play. You can add on your own touches, like our rule on the Leather Wedge tour that you can kick the ball once each round. Or add in a couple of celebrity drops/mulligans to just ease the pressure a little. In fact, there's nothing stopping you doing it entirely your own way ...

I think the most wonderful example I know of a person playing golf to their own tune and no one else's goes to my father-in-law, John. John just loves the game of golf ... brought up in a tiny mining village in Scotland, he's lived and breathed golf from the earliest age, caddying for his father on the beautiful local course before learning himself. So, it's really been a lifelong passion for him, and he's become a real expert of the game, knowing more facts and figures than anyone I've ever met. But there is a twist – to put it mildly, my father-in-law has an 'eccentric swing' which seems to excite the ball to travel in all number of unwanted directions. Now, being my wife's father, it may come as no surprise for me to say that he has stubbornly refused all attempts over the years to improve his swing, saying he's perfectly happy with it as it is. But that doesn't stop him wanting to play and to compete. This still matters to him enormously. I learnt this quite forcibly on my first meeting with him, a rather nervy affair early in my 'courtship' of his daughter. John invited me and Helen to play a few holes with him at his local club in Kent. I was delighted and thought this an ideal chance to impress him. But as we walked up the first I learnt that we wouldn't be playing by the 'old' rules, but instead by the scoring system that John had invented himself, which shall we say 'favours' putting skills, in which he more than holds his own, and rather compensates for all those inconvenient, less important shots it might take to reach the green. The upshot was that I found myself being soundly beaten by the ninth hole, despite taking approximately half the conventional shots. With a slight smile on his lips, my future father-in-law asked me how I liked his scoring system. In the circumstances, with my girlfriend looking rather pointedly at me, I had no hesitation in saying that I thought it a fine system indeed.

And you know what, despite it bringing me down a peg or two, it is a fine system, in fact, it's an ideal system for beginner golfers, those with no handicap, or who tend to drive short or who rely on their putting to get them through a game. Bear with me, it's a bit complicated, but basically John awards 1 point for getting your ball onto the fairway (even if it's only gone 50 yards), awards a second point for the longest drive, and two more points for getting it on the green in net regulation. This means, that before he hits the green, John can typically pick up a point, which is a good start. Once on the green, he awards 2 points for putting in for one, and 1 point for a two putt. So, he can pick up another 2 points here if he's lucky, bringing his score for the typical hole to a more than passable 3, which in Stableford terms would probably still be a 0. Playing against a better golfer, who might pick up 2 points on the way to the green and 1 point when on it, you can see that it even things up. The system provides a morale boost, a shot of confidence, positivity and some self-respect to all those many many golfers out there who love to compete, but whose game typically leaves them trailing.

So, to sum up, tear up your conventional score card, and enjoy talking to your friends, appreciating the view and the walk. And if you value playing 'well', then go ahead and measure it, but make sure you do it John's way – in fact, scrap that, do it your way.

CHAPTER TWELVE

Bottomless Socks

What not to learn

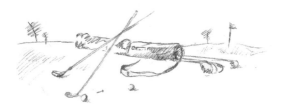

As I believe I've mentioned (!) my wife is very ambitious and very stubborn. This is both a blessing and a curse. For example, when she wanted to learn to knit, her first project was not a scarf like everyone else in the group, but a sock. When she decided to learn the art of pottery, she told the teacher she'd like to make a full tea set, starting with the teapot. Neither were successful ... she made one heel-less sock and gave up, and her teapot evolved into a lopsided bowl that is somewhere in the dark recesses of a cupboard.

I very much admire my wife's drive and passion, but with knitting and pottery – much like golf – there are some things that you need to learn to do really well first before you can go ahead and do the more complicated stuff. My wife now neither knits nor potters, having given both up in a fit of pique after these unsuccessful beginnings ... and there are very many failed golfers who have given up for a similar reason: they either had unrealistic expectations or focused on the wrong things early in their learning, making it very difficult for them to succeed. It might sound boring, but there's something to be said for mastering the basics.

What does a golf pro and a hairdresser have in common? We are both very likely to encounter clients who want things that we cannot deliver! For hairdressers, this is likely to be clients asking to look like a celebrity or to have their straight hair made curly, or their thin hair thick ... now maybe hairstyling has evolved and these things are possible, but I suspect there are still heart-sink moments when a client asks for something unobtainable.

It's much the same for golf tuition – to pick just a few, I've had a well-known actress request to learn golf with the proviso that she be competent in two weeks – in time to go away with a new boyfriend on a golf holiday. I've also had a music producer who wanted to cut his handicap in two but would only commit to practice once a week, and the businesswoman who wanted to channel the swing of Michelle Wee. I love and respect all my clients, and will always do my best, but tuition is not a panacea, and in these circumstances I tend not to mince my words ... If I don't think my client has a realistic or helpful goal, I'll tell them. I wonder if I'd be so brave if I were a hairdresser?

So, with honestly in mind, here are just a few of the things that I'm commonly asked to teach which I don't think are worth worrying about. I share them with you here in the hope that it will save you a bit of time and misplaced effort.

Don't sweat the small stuff

There are some things that are right at the centre of learning golf, and some things on the periphery. I think for any beginner or improver it's important to focus attention on the central principles that are within your control and will result in you being able to get out and play the game as quickly as possible. I'm talking here about keeping the focus on creating a free flowing and reliable swing. Anything else is a bit of a red herring and could cause unnecessary frustration and delay in learning the game.

And that's about what I said to a prospective client who came to *Urban Golf* specifically wanting to work on his set up and grip. He said he'd been playing on and off for a few years and had recently started to concentrate on perfecting what is commonly known as the 'golfing fundamentals' and wanted to book a series of lessons to cement this learning. I told him that I was happy to help him but that it would only take 10 minutes to deal with this area of learning, and there'd be no need to have a whole lesson on it, let alone the series of lessons that he'd been proposing.

He seemed rather put out that I wouldn't take his money and do the 'deep dive' on his grip and set up that he'd been looking for, and thought I was over-simplifying something really important. He took out a copy of Ben Hogan's classic book, *Five Lessons: The Modern Fundamentals of Golf*, and began by showing me the many detailed drawings of the set up and then the eighteen pages focused on establishing the grip, emphasising the opening quote *A good swing starts with a good grip*.

Now, far be it from me to disagree with Ben Hogan, and the way he chooses to portray these starting points – his grip, stance and posture are indeed fine examples of how to prepare to hit the ball – but it's the centrality of them to successful play that I'm not so sure about. If we take the grip as an example, Hogan himself began playing golf with a different grip to that of his book and managed to play very nicely long before he decided to change it and then talk about it in his book. So maybe the grip was an important part of him reaching heights of international excellence, but it certainly wasn't the key to him being able to play good golf in the first place.

Similarly, for me in my naivety as a beginner golfer I

just set myself up to hit the ball in a way that felt comfortable and gripped the club in what I now know was a very unorthodox manner with my right hand above my left. And I could still swing the club, play golf and gain my first handicap, only swapping to a more conventional grip when it came under scrutiny from other club members.

So, for the majority of golfers who play for fun, the key to the set up and grip is to establish a way of standing and holding the club that feels comfortable and natural and allows you to swing the club. The exact details of how you stand, how wide your legs are placed, whether you adopt Hogan's recommended grip, a baseball grip, or that favoured by Tiger Woods, I don't think matters very much. The key is to find a position that works for you and quickly move on to learning the key principles of golf that will really make a difference to your game.

I said much of this to my prospective client, who wasn't entirely convinced but agreed to demonstrate to me his current set up and grip. It took him what seemed like several minutes of adjusting and readjusting his hands and awkwardly moulding his body into a position for him to feel ready to swing his club. And, I must say, it was an impressive 'looking' set up with a picture-perfect grip, straight out of the pages of any golfing text book, let alone Hogan's. I told him so and said that I couldn't see anything that needed work. But then, in true Columbo style, I dropped in one further question ... *Are you comfortable?* I asked. He looked up at me surprised and frowned, *I'm not sure*, he replied, *should I be?*

And therein lay the problem, so focused had this client been on setting up correctly, that he'd forgotten or overlooked the need to feel comfortable. With the set up and grip, really the only priority is to be comfortable and balanced – because it is this relaxed yet dynamic starting point that allows the swing to move freely, consistently and powerfully. The tension within an overly contrived 'perfect' set-up stops the free-flowing movement before it starts.

So, in the end, we did have a lesson focused on the grip and set up. But if anything, we worked on de-perfecting it, approaching the body as a relaxed base for the swing to move through and the club as a friend to be held rather than as a precious object to be revered. Soon my new client looked a lot more comfortable and natural, and told me he'd never swung the club as well in his life. And so perhaps Ben Hogan was right, and the grip is the key to the swing ... but not always in the way he envisaged.

Look after the chicken and you'll get an egg

I don't mind what it takes. In fact, if you ask me to come for lessons every day, I will. The fact of the matter is I want you to teach me the secrets to the golf swing so I can swing the club and hit the ball as perfectly straight as the pros do. So said Richard, an enthusiastic twenty-year-old student at the LSE, keen to gain entry to the university's esteemed golf team.

Now this wasn't the first nor probably the last time I'm likely to hear this request from a client. And you could argue it's a fair one considering so many golfers have been led to believe that the very best players possess some sort of mythical ability to hit the ball perfectly long and straight down the middle of the fairway. And of course, it's in our natures to then want to try and obtain some of these skills for ourselves, however out of reach they may seem to be. I hated to burst this young man's bubble, but the truth is that it is really rare for a ball to fly perfectly straight down a fairway, more of a happy accident than a schooled and reliable habit. I had to let him know that any effort we put into pursuing this aim would be a waste of energy, time and the limited resources he had to pay me for his lessons.

I could see his eyes dull and his shoulders sag. I felt terrible. The last thing I wanted to do was crush his wonderful enthusiasm for the game. So, I went on quickly and told him that the good thing was that most of the best players aren't actually trying to hit the ball perfectly straight anyway, but instead have worked on establishing a swing that will enable the ball to finish straight. *Ok ok, go on*, he said, encouraged. I explained that there is a vast difference between the two ... a golfer trying to hit the ball straight will be continually disappointed, and forever consumed with trying to fix each and every wayward shot, confining them to a life of frustrating visits to the range and an unwanted addiction to the internet. Worse still, it's highly probable that they won't end up finding any prolonged consistency to their swing.

However, I said, looking at him encouragingly, golfers who school and refine their own reliable swing will likely have a consistent shape to it. And regardless of whether that's a fade, a draw, a hook or even a slice, believe me, they are more likely to be able to predict where their ball will start and finish and so play well on the course.

Thinking he needed some more convincing, I led him away from the playing space and sat down with him in front of one of *Urban Golf's* large TV screens, which was currently playing the Open championship. I asked Richard to watch a few holes with me, paying particular attention to the pro tracer used to highlight the balls flight and trajectory. I offered him a wager that if he actually saw any ball fly perfectly straight, I would take on his challenge for free. And if he didn't, he'd agree to drop his original aim, and come back and have some lessons with me to establish his own consistently shaped swing.

Suffice to say, he was back the following week, and within three lessons he'd established a sweet, simple fade that consistently got his ball finishing down the middle of the fairway.

Experienced Golfers Only

There are no secrets or shortcuts in golf. The best players in the world got there because they took total command and ownership of the basic and uncomplicated fundamentals of golf and schooled them to a level of excellence that most of us can only dream of.

In fact, I would propose this be true for men and women at the top of any sport. The best techniques have evolved from years of dedication to practising the basic techniques over and over again, building up thousands and thousands of hours of muscle and mind memories from which to draw.

And when you have this kind of deep well of knowledge and well grooved pattern of movement, it makes sense that you are then able to consider your sport in very minute and complex detail, making subtle almost imperceptible changes and adjustments to further improve and strengthen technique. What results is the wonderful illusion of something magical and effortless.

But it is an illusion, and there's no quick or easy way to reach the level of excellence only achieved through a lifetime of practice. But of course, this isn't a message particularly palatable in our society. We're used to getting things quickly and easily – I can order something online to be delivered to my house the same day, I can read a condensed online newspaper in five minutes and have a hot meal in three.

I do think that the pace and restlessness of the culture of our age makes it incredibly hard to accept and embrace learning over time – small, imperceptible improvements and change over months and years rather than hours and days. And I think this need for speed can 'infect' our approach to sports like golf, with golf publications both online and in print often offering quick fixes, secret techniques and breakthrough technologies as the answer to improving one's game, possibly to the cost of just putting in some more practice hours and getting out on the course.

Perhaps the clearest manifestation of this for me is in the use and misuse of high-speed video analysis. This technology developed as a way to further dissect and discover the intricate details of the best players techniques, but is now widely used on driving ranges and by golf pros to record and play back in excruciating detail the swings of all their clients, often offering the facility to split the screen, to compare the clients swing with a famous golfer of their choice.

Now this scrutiny has its place. For the experienced golfer who is already competent and well-schooled in the swing fundamentals, this technology offers the chance to capture the finer grain detail of the swings' progression, allowing more complex and subtle improvements to be made.

But for the rest of us, it provides information way beyond what we are able to process and take on board, exacerbating the illusion that the expert's swing is within reach if only we make this and that adjustment and shift this, slow down here etc. Even if this were the answer – which I think it evidently is not – there's no way we could make the changes needed to deliver them through the swing without a deep well of knowledge and experience to drawn upon.

So, my fear which unfortunately is borne out by my experience, is that for beginner and improving golfers, this technology takes focus away from the teaching and practicing of the basic principles that are within the golfers control. It also shifts the focus of learning to the appearance of the swing rather than to how it feels in the body and mind. This kind of quick fix approach to accessing an expert swing is likely to delay or prevent improvement rather than facilitate it.

If you can keep your head when all about you are losing theirs

Kipling just about sums it up in this line. In our modern culture there is so much written on how best to live our lives, and it can all be incredibly tempting and alluring. Be it the latest fitness craze, healthy eating plan, way to organise our lives or conduct our relationships, it's very difficult to decipher which are actually important lessons and which take us away from ourselves and the things that matter most to us.

And so with golf, I guess if there's something to take from my list of things not to learn, it's to try not to get caught up in the peripheral stuff, or strive for technique beyond your reach or fall for quick fixes. Just enjoy the fundamentals ... Learn to swing the club in a way that feels fluid and smooth and grounded and right for you. And once you feel comfortable with your swing, golf opens up to you. Now you can begin to practice all the different long and short shots that the course offers and you can have fun practicing and experimenting and finding your own ways to play the game. It's as simple or as complicated as that.

Final word to Jack Nicholas, who knows a thing or two about how to play golf: *Golf is a game where you have to understand yourself. You have to understand what your abilities are and you have to play within your abilities. If you get outside of that, that's when you get beat.*

CHAPTER THIRTEEN

The Uncorrupted Pleasure of an Old Bladed Putter

Just living and putting

1979
Shakedown 1979, cool kids never have the time,
On a live wire right up off the street
You and I should meet,
June bug skipping like a stone,
With the headlights pointed at the dawn,
We were sure we'd never see an end to it all

The Smashing Pumpkins, from the 1996
album *Mellon Collie and the Infinite Sadness.*

For my sixteenth birthday my uncle very kindly gave to me his old Bobby Locke Slazenger bladed putter. I remember thinking that it was the most beautiful club that I had ever seen. Long and sleek, it had a small but perfect silver head. The blade was a very popular club back in the day when Jack Nicklaus won fifteen of his eighteen majors with the George Low Wizard 600 blade. But by the time I got mine, they were fast becoming outdated and replaced by the more playable style of mallet putter. To me though, it didn't matter, I adored it from the first.

The love I gave that club. Carefully polishing it after each round, rewrapping it in its snug cover, and keeping it in view propped up against my wardrobe, ready at a moment's notice for a little putting practice along the well scuffed ridge of carpet in my bedroom. Me and my Bobby Locke were inseparable for 20 years, and became very good friends. It felt so comfortable and natural to hold and play, as if it had been made just for me. I'd still be playing with it now if I could, but after such long and dedicated service first to my uncle, and then to me – not all of it kind I must admit – it's a bit bent, and the bladed design demands regular practice and play. I just can't commit to that now in my life.

This might seem hopelessly nostalgic, but I think of my Bobby Locke with such fondness and high regard it brings back so many wonderful memories of my teens and twenties, a time of my life that was so happy, so carefree, with few responsibilities, plenty of time, I just lived and breathed golf like oxygen. Now don't get me wrong, I love my life now, with the complex layers of joy and pain which come with the demands of having a young family, a mortgage, a marriage, and a much greater awareness of the difficulties and fragility of the world beyond my fortunate boundaries. But there was something about those times, so simple, uncorrupted by worry, doubt, advice or judgment – I was just living and putting! So, indulge me if you will as I share with you some of my favourite memories of the times Bobby Locke and I shared in those heady days of the late 80s and 90s.

Complete Trust

You know what it's like when you spend time with a really old and really good friend, the conversation moves so effortlessly as the texture of the years of shared memories allows you to understand where they're coming from, what they value, who they really are. There's few surprises, you don't necessarily get that fizz of expectation you can experience with a newer friend, but what you do get is a trust so deep and solid that you know they'll be there for you whenever and forever – they've got your back.

And so it was with my Bobby Locke. We spent so many hours over so many years practising together, that the grip became formed to my hand, the shaft became an extension of my arm and my body and the club felt so connected that we instantly and naturally arranged our bodies to commune with one another. I was lucky to have the time and space to develop such a close and familiar arrangement with my putter, and it's something that I now encourage my clients to find with theirs – to get to know and understand their putter, and to set themselves up to fit the design of their particular putter rather than to take a 'standard' position.

Of course, it wasn't like this from the beginning. I remember early on that my new Bobby Locke seemed strange and alien, demanding so much more precision that my borrowed putter had asked of me. The Bobby Locke didn't suffer fools gladly and made it abundantly clear to me that I'd need to put in a bit of effort if I wanted to work with him. And so I did. Hours and hours and hours. It was never a chore, I simply loved the sensation of the delicate stroke, the soft feel of the ball as it made contact with the silver head and the irresistible sound like an ice cube dropping into a glass as the ball fell into the hole. Every Saturday I used to rock up at Chesham & Ley Hill GC, play eighteen holes with some of the other juniors, laughing, joking and probably annoying the older members, as we ambled noisily and slowly around the course. I'd then have a Coke and get on the putting green, plug in my

Walkman and listen to Duran Duran whilst practicing 3-foot putts, taking time before each putt to visualise its path into the hole before attempting to execute it. Over time the discrepancy between what I thought the putt would do and what actually happened narrowed, and my success rate improved. This kind of visualisation is still a technique I use and encourage my clients to do to this day. I'd practice putts from below and above the hole, on a ridge, from a funny angle, again and again and again. I used to invent mini competitions to keep myself motivated, seeing how many putts I could hole out of a 100. After a few months my score was regularly up in the 90s, but you know for all the years I practiced that drill, I never got that elusive 100/100 score line ... Which was probably the thing that kept me practising.

So engrained did the 3-foot putt become in my body and mind that I came to trust it implicitly, feeling so confident and sure of the shot, that I've managed to sustain that feeling my whole life, during putting droughts, big tournaments, successes and disappointments. Why I practised just that distance, I'm not sure. I think one of the members had told me that if I could be confident over the shorter putts, the longer ones would look after themselves. And of course, he was so right, practicing longer putts has limited impact as there are so many contingencies that you can't really prepare for each and every eventuality and you also have a pretty high chance of missing, and practicing a putt you're more than likely to miss is not necessarily the best way to build confidence! Instead, I found that having full trust in my short range putts meant I could approach the longer putts without fear of the consequences, because I knew that even if I missed and was left with a dreaded downhill left to right return putt, I'd got it in the bag – or more accurately – the hole.

The best of times

There was a summer in the mid-90s that I look back on as one of the best in my life. I had moved out of my parent's home and was living in an amazing shared house with some of my closest friends and was in love with a wonderful girl. Music, partying, garden cricket and golf were at the top of my agenda. As with most things in life, the happiness of that summer was bittersweet, made more poignant by the sense that this couldn't last forever … My girlfriend was shortly leaving for university, one of my house mates was moving out to live with his girlfriend, another would leave shortly for a 'proper' job in London. There was a real sense in the air that this was our last summer all together, and we had to make the most of it. One of my favourite memories of that summer was of me and my housemates entering the Hazlemere pro-am golf tournament. We were all pretty decent amateurs at this point, and I pulled in a close friend of mine and pro down in Bournemouth to join us. The rest of our 'gang' were invited to either caddy, carry the beers or just follow us round to create a crowd. As a one off, my girlfriend agreed to caddy for me – a huge honour ... she wasn't generally a big fan of golf.

We entered purely for the fun of being all together and playing the game that we loved. We had a few sneaky beers on the way round and were just relaxed, happy and cared little for the outcome. And as so often when you don't try too hard, things just kept coming off – our drives were long and straight, when one friend missed another holed and we even made a miraculous eagle 2 on the par-four tenth. With everyone on a high, laughing, joking, reminiscing, the birdies kept coming and we began to wake up to thinking that we could actually win this thing. We knew 18 under par would give us a chance of victory and by the sixteenth we were 17 under. One more birdie would surely be enough to win the cup.

With the smell of victory now clearly in the air, we stood on the par-three seventeenth buzzing with excitement – so much so that my team mates lost it a bit and I was the only one that managed to make it onto the green, but even then my ball was still some 18 foot from the hole. One of my three team mates went on to secure a par, so we needed one more par from me to keep our hopes for victory alive, which meant getting this tricky putt down in two.

My girlfriend passed me my Bobby Locke and I examined the putt ... gauging the distance, the roll, the break ... I looked over at my friends. They looked nervous ... *Don't three-putt it!* writ large on their faces. But then I glanced over to my girlfriend, who was leaning nonchalantly on my bag, looking at me with a slight smile on her lips. We'd been together about a year at this point and she was everything to me. She'd introduced me to chess, to the classics and to a world I didn't know existed, we were in love like only young people can be, with an intensity that predicted our shared knowing that this was likely to be our last few weeks together. I smiled back at her, and very suddenly it was crystal clear to me that I was going to hole the putt. I remember the incredible calm I felt in my body as I pictured exactly what I needed to do, and my Bobby Locke seemed to effortlessly create the exact movement I imagined, and obligingly the ball rolled smoothly down the slope, breaking at just the right point before disappearing into the hole.

I don't remember much of our cup-winning cele-brations that night, but the memory burns bright in my mind of my girlfriend on that seventeenth green flinging her arms around my neck and screaming in my ear, before the boys piled round, slapping my back and ruffling my hair. It was the best of times, and the end of times, truly halcyon days.

The worst of times

I've had plenty of good putting days in my golfing life – some great – and a fair few dismal ones as well.

170

Annoyingly, it's true when they say that it's the bad days that teach us the most. The putting nightmare I remember the most vividly turned out to be a pretty important day for me as I was given a piece of golfing wisdom that has stayed with me all these years, but I still wince when I think of some of those putts!

It was way back when I was an amateur playing at Harewood Downs in Buckinghamshire. I was a student at the time, and only had about four lectures a week, so I had plenty of time to devote to my golf. Most months I'd take part in the informal 'mid-week medal', where club members would team up to play the eighteen-hole competition. On the day in question, I was pleased to be teamed up with my friend Arnold, a long-standing member of the club and a wonderful golfer with a handicap of seven, which isn't bad I guess for a man who must have been in his seventies.

I don't know what was in the air that day, but for some reason, nothing seemed to work for me. My drives were short, my chips were wayward, but my putting, oh my goodness, my putting was a travesty. It was almost as if I had entered some kind of Dali-esque painting where the normal is distorted and strange, and the holes were too small and my balls were suddenly square edged and too big to stand a chance. After five holes, I was something like ten shots over my handicap, having three-putted the first, three-putted the second and three-putted the fifth. I was angry, humiliated and looking for someone or something to blame. I think it was on the ninth hole, after posting another disastrous double bogey, that I threw my poor Bobby Locke into the dense woodland adjoining the course, accompanied by the melodramatic musing, *What is happening to me!* It was only then that Arnold stepped in. Now Arnold was not one of those club members desperate to offer his advice and expertise at the drop of a hat. He was a thoughtful and quiet man, and very respectful of the games of others, but I think he could see I needed something to calm me down.

He fished my Bobby Locke out of the bush I'd deposited it in, handed it back to me, and calmly said to me, *James my boy, it's just not your day.* Now this might not sound like a transformative profundity on first reading, but in this phrase is a kernel of truth so key that it's a central part of what I teach to this day. Arnold went on to tell me that with golf, but particularly with putting, there are just some days when it doesn't work. It's almost like there's some special button on the putter that gets switched to the off position, taking away the fluidity, feel and accuracy of the stroke. Crucially, Arnold told me that it happens to all golfers, without exception, some regularly, whilst others are lucky to only have their putting turned 'off' maybe once or twice in their career.

Arnold said that the key thing to do is to do nothing at all ... to just accept that it's perfectly normal, not a problem and to not beat yourself up or spend excessive time analysing what has gone wrong. He told me of a friend of his who had one of these 'off' days and had literally never recovered his putting stroke, so focused had he become on finding the solution through a host of different techniques, that he'd developed the feared golfing malady called the 'yips'. And Arnold's diagnosis? That this poor man's brain had simply got in the way of his body.

Anyway, I got through the rest of the round. I didn't play much better on the back nine, my putts were still determinedly staying above ground, but my mind was a lot calmer. I wasn't panicking any more, and that was reflected in a less dismal final score. I'll forever be grateful for Arnold pulling me out of my putting nightmare that day, and still hold on to that simple wisdom, *it's just not your day*, to carry me through difficult times, whether it be in golf or in life.

All this talk of my Bobby Locke got me fishing about in the back of my wardrobe last weekend to find my old friend and reunite him with my bag of clubs. I'd arranged to play a few holes with a friend, who just happened to be one of the gang at Hazlemere all those years ago. It's funny how 'truth' is such a personal concept. My friend's overriding memory of that day was of how he had saved the tournament with an audacious pitch in at the fourteenth, but there we go, I'll give him that. I played pretty well that evening, and the

Bobby Locke did me proud, holing a 15-footer on the fourth for a birdie, and making some satisfying 3-footers to save par. My friend and I had a beer and chatted happily as we ambled round, the sun was warm and heavy in the sky, and for a few hours my responsibilities drifted away, and I was transported back to those endless, carefree summers of the 1990s.

About the author

James Ellis-Caird is a PGA professional golf coach, a husband, father, first time dog owner and lover of homemade baking.

James was captivated by the game of golf after striking his first shot with a borrowed five iron at Chesham and Ley Hill GC. Thirty-five years later his love affair with the game is going strong, channeling his passion into making golf more accessible, more open and more enjoyable for everyone.

After living all his life in Buckinghamshire, James, his wife and 8-year-old son have recently moved to the North Yorkshire coastline, with the dream to start a smallholding, play some beautiful golf courses, surf some waves and eat lots of fish and chips.

A late comer to the world of social media, James has recently found a new passion in content creation, with his videos and pictures encapsulating the beauty of the game he loves.

To follow James and his adventures, you can find him on Instagram –

https://www.instagram.com/rewilding_the_golfer/